JÜRGEN KLOPP

NOTES ON A SEASON

JÜRGEN KLOPP

NOTES ON A SEASON

Reach Sport
www.reachsport.com

First published in Great Britain in 2020 by
Reach Sport, 5 St Paul's Square, Liverpool, L3 9SJ.

www.reachsport.com
@reach_sport

Reach Sport is a part of Reach plc.
One Canada Square, Canary Wharf, London, E15 5AP.

ISBN: 978-1-911613-77-0

Compiled by: Roy Gilfoyle
Artwork by: Rick Cooke

Printed and bound by CPI Group (UK) Ltd,
Croydon, CR0 4YY.

NOTES ON A SEASON

2019-20

INSPIRED BY ADVERSITY, KLOPP'S MEN SET A RELENTLESS PACE TO TURN DOUBTERS INTO BELIEVERS

THERE are two ways to react to adversity: you can accept your failings and crumble or come back stronger.

Anyone who has ever worked with Jürgen Norbert Klopp will tell you there was only one of those options he was ever likely to strive for after his team were pipped to the Premier League title in May 2019.

The charismatic Liverpool manager had built a side that had taken the Reds to their best ever haul of points in a season, but 97 of them still weren't enough to beat a formidable rival in Manchester City.

A time like that can test the most loyal of supporters. After 29 years of waiting, if the third highest points total in English top-flight history can't win you the thing you want most, maybe the Premier League title would always remain tantalisingly beyond your reach?

This was the key moment. Was Klopp surrounded by doubters or believers?

"We can decide how we deal with that," Klopp said after his team finished the season with a 2-0 win over Wolves. "If we are ready to make the next step, we will make the next step. That's the plan from tomorrow on."

If anybody in the stands still had any doubts, the reaction of his squad suggested the players believed they could control their own destiny and turn outstanding performances on the pitch into tangible reward.

Klopp and his men proved their resolve three weeks later.

A year on from losing the UEFA Champions League final to Real Madrid, they could celebrate winning Europe's biggest prize themselves, keeping their nerve to overcome Tottenham in Madrid.

Winning the European Cup and seeing Liverpool city centre packed with delirious, celebrating fans proved this wasn't a squad of nearly men and whetted the appetite for more success.

Against such a high-calibre opponent, the Reds would need to raise the bar even higher and Klopp's team set about breaking records of their own.

The stall was set out in the first Premier League game of the season, racing into a 4-0 half-time lead against Norwich, and by the end of August, Jordan Henderson had shimmied his way to lifting the UEFA Super Cup.

The Reds won their first eight Premier League matches to surge to the top of the table and by Christmas had only dropped two points, setting a relentless pace.

Highlights were many but the 2-1 win at Aston Villa showed that Klopp's 'mentality monsters' never give up, equalising in the 86th minute before forcing an injury-time winner. Then the 4-0 Boxing Day win at high-flying Leicester, just days after Klopp's men had become club world champions in Doha, let everyone know that Liverpool were the team to beat.

Excitement grew that the club's 30-year wait for a league title might soon come to an end, with the Kop frequently belting out 'we're gonna win the league' as home wins came and went, and Klopp knew a vital part of his job was to keep everyone's feet on the ground.

"They [the fans] are allowed to dream, to sing, whatever they want," he said. "We will not be part of that party yet because we know our job."

The Reds wouldn't suffer a league defeat until the last day of February but a unique season took a terrible turn the following month as the global coronavirus pandemic put football on hold.

Klopp became a spokesman for his club and his sport, putting football in perspective; then three months later he and the staff faced the new challenge of preparing the squad to restart the season.

Despite carrying a 25-point lead, Klopp wouldn't let his side rest on their laurels and a 4-0 win over Crystal Palace, followed by City's defeat at Chelsea, meant the race had been won. Liverpool were English league winners for the first time in three decades. The Liverbird was back on its perch – with a record seven games left to play. Seven guards of honour to enjoy.

World champions, European champions and league champions at the same time.

Klopp and his team had shown they were ready to take the next step.

Now relive a remarkable season through the words of a remarkable manager.

AUG

2019

A Community Shield defeat to Manchester City at Wembley gave Jürgen Klopp an early taster of what he was up against if he wanted to go one better than the 2018/19 season. The Liverpool manager knew that every point would be precious when the league campaign got underway

9th: Norwich City (PL) H
14th: Chelsea (SC) N
17th: Southampton (PL) A
24th: Arsenal (PL) H
31st: Burnley (PL) A

v Norwich City
Friday, August 9th, 8pm

'THIS SEASON PROVIDES THE BEST KIND OF OPPORTUNITY FOR ALL OF US IN THE LFC FOLD'

Premier League

GOOD evening and welcome back to Anfield for the first Premier League fixture of the new season against Norwich City.

I would like to start these notes by offering congratulations to our visitors today on their amazing achievement of last season – winning promotion as champions in one of the toughest domestic leagues there is.

I have never managed in the Championship but I follow it closely, predominantly because we often have young players on loan there – but also because my friend David Wagner achieved promotion with Huddersfield. David often spoke about the intense, relentless nature of it and how you have to have a team with the strongest mentality to endure it and be successful.

I welcome Daniel Farke, his players, staff, officials and supporters of Norwich City to Anfield tonight.

It's not just that he achieved promotion but how the team did it that deserves so much praise for Daniel. They are brave, they are adventurous, they are organised, they are resilient. So many late and dramatic wins. They are a group who knows what it is like to win – believe in what they do – and they now have amazing shared experiences.

This is a very dangerous opponent. Tonight I have no doubt they'll be on fire.

I'm sure the away end will be full of bright colours and noise tonight as well. So, for us – as Liverpool – we know our job. We need to be better in all departments.

A new season is always about opportunity. I think this coming one presents the best kind of opportunity for all of us in the LFC fold.

As the team, we know we have the opportunity to be better than we were last season. This I love about football. Regardless of what came before you know there are new challenges and new memories to make.

This team, since I have been fortunate enough to lead them, has been all about progression collectively and individually. They know standing still means you actually fall backwards.

The Premier League, the domestic cups and Europe – all our opponents will make strides forward. Our strides can and must be bigger if we want to achieve.

I hear the words often, after a season like we just had, about how difficult or how important it is to 'go again'. I don't dislike the sentiment and there is merit to it, but simply 'going again' won't be enough. We need to be even stronger, even fitter, smarter, more committed, greater focus.

Maybe a slight change on the sentiment: 'improve again', maybe 'progress again'.

Here is what I know for certain: it will be the toughest, most challenging season we will all face, and that is because of the quality we compete with. Starting tonight we face outstanding players, led by brilliant managers and coaches week in and week out – it doesn't stop. But it's the challenge that makes it so fulfilling and so enjoyable. Let's never lose sight of what we are all involved in; it's about energy and joy, it's about shared experiences. There is so much in the outside world that is not to enjoy at the moment, so much that is divisive. Football at its best is the antidote to this, albeit we know it can only often be brief respite.

Football offers the chance for people from all backgrounds and all communities to come together and focus on achieving something amazing through collective effort.

Everyone – from the players to the staff to the supporters – shares equally in the joyous moment of a goal or a win. We can all experience the fulfilment that comes from helping each other. Supporters give energy to the players through atmosphere and players give energy back through their commitment and enterprise. Everyone contributes and everyone benefits.

These are the values that will shape our season. If we all look to continue this relationship – of one big community, all coming together to help the team achieve – then we can enjoy special moments again I think.

If I had one message for the coming season, to everyone who cares about this amazing club, it is that we are ready for some great times if we are prepared to work together to achieve it. We can stay together at all times if we want it this way, good times and bad.

As the team, management and players, we know what our responsibilities are and we are hungry and eager to deliver more. We know our supporters will be the wind at our backs.

The rest is about the journey and making sure you take all the joy you can from the moment.

This evening we are back at Anfield, our home. Let's cherish every moment we have in this special place together and focus entirely on this game and giving all we have to win and then enjoy that feeling together.

Liverpool 4, Norwich City 1

Goals: Hanley (7og), Salah (19), Van Dijk (28), Origi (42)

Line-up (4-3-3): Alisson (Adrian 39), Alexander-Arnold, Gomez, Van Dijk, Robertson, Fabinho, Henderson (c), Wijnaldum, Salah, Firmino (Milner 86), Origi (Mane 74). Subs not used: Keita, Oxlade-Chamberlain, Shaqiri, Matip

Jürgen's post-match reaction: 'Good. For a long part of the game, really good. I think the first 60 minutes were pretty impressive. If you are surprised that Norwich use little moments for being dangerous as well, I'm not – that's how they are. That's really good and still for 60 minutes we did what we had to do. We had to defend a couple of times in the last moment. Passion makes a difference in these moments, that's what you have to show and I liked the work-rate we put in and the respect we showed them.'

Wednesday, August 14th, 8pm
UEFA Super Cup,
Liverpool 2, Chelsea 2 (after extra time, Liverpool win 5-4 on penalties)
Besiktas Arena

Goals: Mane (48, 95)

Line-up (4-3-3): Adrian, Gomez, Matip, Van Dijk, Robertson (Alexander-Arnold 90), Fabinho, Henderson (c), Milner (Wijnaldum 64), Salah, Mane (Origi 103), Oxlade-Chamberlain (Firmino 45). Subs not used: Lonergan, Kelleher, Lallana, Shaqiri, Brewster, Hoever, Elliott

Klopp was in jubilant mood after winning the club's fourth UEFA Super Cup following a penalty shoot-out.

On his players being able to touch the 'This is Anfield' sign after winning two European trophies...

Actually we don't have time for that! We play on Saturday again, we have to find a way to be ready for that game.

After 90 minutes, I think, when it was close to the final whistle, Frank Lampard asked me: 'Where do you play and when do you play [at the weekend]?'

And I said 'Southampton on Saturday – congratulations!' Nobody wanted extra-time tonight, they play

Leicester at home on Sunday but they played last Sunday so there was no advantage tonight but for the next game for both it will be pretty tough. But we have to be ready again and that's my present to the players to help them recover so that they are ready for the game. It was a big fight tonight and I didn't know before the game how good it would be when you win it, but it's brilliant, it's really big. The atmosphere in the stadium was outstanding, it showed us again how big this club is: wherever we go, our supporters are already there. I don't know exactly how many fans were from Istanbul but I can only say 'thank you' because it was just a brilliant atmosphere. We would have loved to bring our weather to Turkey for one day at least because it was really intense, but now it's done, we came through and we won it. The boys feel really good, I feel really good, so everything is okay.

On being the first German manager to win the Super Cup and whether that will have an impact on other coaches from his homeland...

I didn't know that and I never thought about things like that in my whole life. It's nice, there must be a first one so I'm sure I'm not the last one. There are a lot of good coaches in Germany but it's nice to be there, but I don't see myself as German really. I am German and I like that but I see myself more as European and I felt like that again tonight. That when we all have the same targets we are so close to each other, in parts of life it looks sometimes that we have different ideas, different targets, but as people we are all the same. We all want the same and when we have something so wonderful like loving Liverpool FC, then it shows that we could really be much closer together than we are in reality. So it's not about me winning it, it's about LFC winning it, winning it for all the people who support us and I can feel how much it meant to all these people and that makes me really happy.

On what it means to lift the Super Cup…

I asked Millie and Hendo after the game, 'how do people see it?' I'm not long enough in the country and was never in that game before. They said, 'Oh no, it's a proper trophy'. It's on a wall at Melwood, so good. They have to draw it again, to paint the wall at Melwood again, bring another number on the wall '2019' and a picture of whatever. I didn't know before the game how big it would feel. Now I know it and it's great. But it's not about me – I don't only say that, I mean that – it's really about doing it for the people. From four opportunities in the last three months, we won two. That's good, that's absolutely okay.

Now let's carry on. Let's try to find a way to win on Saturday and let's try to find a way in the game after. Southampton, Arsenal is coming up and both will be incredibly difficult for different reasons. I think the only team that celebrated more tonight than us is probably Southampton when they saw '90 minutes, no decision, let them go again'. But we will have to find a way to win the game. I have a couple of hours to think about that and that's what I will do after talking to all of you.

On the display and story of Adrian...

I don't know where Adrian was two weeks ago when we played Man City! When I spoke to him for the first time, he told me he had a goalie coach. It was clear he would need time to get fit. But we didn't have that time, so he has to be fit now and he was fit. He played an incredible game, he had sensational saves. Both goalies had that, but maybe from Adrian it's a bit more surprising because without pretty much any preparation.

He's not only on the pitch a great person, he showed me already that he's a proper personality in the dressing room as well. He was maybe louder than I was at half-time. He was really on his toes and that was good. It's important and it helps us. He deserves that. Of course in penalty shootouts it's always lucky, but the performance over the 120 minutes was incredible. Making the save for the penalty is the icing on the cake and is wonderful. I saw now one time that he could really grab his towel before he started celebrating. That's special as well, so he's obviously quick in mind and knows what he wants to do. He helped us a lot and he can be really proud of what he did tonight.

Saturday, August 17th, 3pm
Premier League
Southampton 1, Liverpool 2

Goals: Mane (45+1), Firmino (71)

Line-up (4-3-3): Adrian, Alexander-Arnold, Matip, Van Dijk, Robertson, Wijnaldum, Milner (c) (Fabinho 74), Oxlade-Chamberlain (Henderson 89), Mane, Firmino, Salah (Origi 79). Subs not used: Lonergan, Gomez, Lallana, Shaqiri

Jürgen's post-match reaction: 'We are not used to winning big things and then coming to Southampton, I really loved how much respect we showed today. I said before the game that this looks like the biggest banana skin in history; everybody is waiting for it and probably all the headlines were written already. I told the boys the headline I would prefer is 'the mentality giants were in town' – that's how I feel it in the moment. The boys did an outstanding job for today, all good, let's go home, recover and start again. Southampton is a good team, they defend well, they are really just difficult to play. Good counter-attacks, good organisation, all that stuff. Last year, we were 1-0 down and won 3-1 right? That was really difficult and this afternoon it was difficult again. I was really impressed with how fresh we looked, in the start especially, just how good we were. We controlled the game, we were fluent, all that stuff and then with the long balls and set-pieces Southampton came up then.'

v Arsenal
Saturday, August 24th, 5.30pm

'THIS GROUP OF PLAYERS DON'T FEAR INTENSITY – IT'S PART OF OUR IDENTITY AS A TEAM'

Premier League

GOOD afternoon and welcome back to Anfield for the Premier League fixture against Arsenal.

I'm often asked whether, as a manager/coach, you can enjoy certain football games on the basis that they're fantastic to watch for the neutral. There's never a straightforward answer to this and 'enjoy' probably isn't the right word, but matches like the one we have today are certainly to be embraced, not feared.

Even before I came to England, games my teams had against Arsenal were always of the highest intensity and excitement. Be it Dortmund or Liverpool, I don't think I have ever faced an Arsenal team that doesn't have the mindset of positivity and adventure.

I think this current Arsenal team might just be the best yet, in terms of quality, and for that reason I think today pitches two of Europe's best against each other. For a football supporter what is there not to enjoy about this? Both sides are packed with talent, pace and personality.

I welcome Unai Emery, his players, staff, officials and supporters of Arsenal to Anfield today.

My respect for Unai as a coach and leader of a club is as high as you can imagine. His CV across Europe is so impressive. I can also relate to his journey here to England because I myself experienced many of the same challenges he will have done in the past 14 months or so.

Adapting to life in the Premier League and England

isn't straightforward, even when you are blessed to be leading a fantastic club with an incredible support network, as both Unai and I are. I think there is zero doubt Arsenal will be even stronger this season compared to last and I say that without even factoring in the impressive and extensive transfer business they have done. They have recruited amazing talent this summer.

It's one of the reasons why I haven't liked the 'external' focus on pre-season being on just a couple of clubs contesting for honours this season. To me this made no sense at all. It's a complete nonsense if you don't view this Arsenal, with this manager, as being one of the best teams in the country.

They have everything required to go the distance and I think it's why we are in for such an exciting season in the Premier League.

The good news for me and the staff here at Liverpool is that our players do not need reminding today that they face a world-class opponent. The character and attitude which the side have shown since reporting back fills me with pride. Once again they are proving that when it comes to mentality they will not be surpassed.

Performance level, for all sides, requires rhythm before you get anywhere near the highest level – but qualities such as mentality and courage can be constant.

What I have seen from my team, since we began at

Wembley in the Community Shield, through to the full-time whistle going at Southampton last weekend, is that they are not allowing the relentless nature of August to impact upon their application or belief.

I mentioned intensity earlier when talking about fixtures against Arsenal. The start to the season has been intensive, yes, but this group of players have embraced that. They don't view intensity as being something to fear. It's actually part of our make-up – it's our identity as a team.

The other factor, from the start of this season, that has given me so much joy, has been once again the ability to absorb and react to setbacks. It's been there early and it will need to remain.

Be it conceding first in matches, such as against Man City or Chelsea, losing a key player during a game to an injury, or just responding to general setbacks during a game, we have shown our best face in our reaction.

We are a side which if, and when, knocked down, has the ability to bounce back off the canvas and be ready to engage again.

There'll be times, both today and during the season, when we face big setbacks and have big hurdles to clear. But with this team I know we will also rise and not sink. This is what I love about them so much.

Finally, the same qualities of embracing the intensity and reacting in the right way to difficult moments 100 per cent applies to our supporters also. From London, to Anfield, over to Istanbul, back to the south coast of England...our fans have been there with us for every second of every game so far. They know their value and their importance and they know how and when they can make the difference.

We can never and will never promise results for them – they're too educated to know this anyway – but they share the mentality of this team and therefore we know that in good times and difficult times this season they'll be with us.

Liverpool 3, Arsenal 1

Goals: Matip (41), Salah (49pen, 58)

Line-up (4-3-3): Adrian, Alexander-Arnold, Matip, Van Dijk, Robertson, Henderson (c), Fabinho, Wijnaldum (Milner 69), Salah, Firmino (Lallana 86), Mane (Oxlade-Chamberlain 77). Subs not used: Kelleher, Gomez, Shaqiri, Origi

Jürgen's post-match reaction: 'I was really happy with a lot of parts of the game; I think everything we did well in the first four games we did tonight for longer, more precise and better tuned. I loved the desire, the passion, the power and the energy that we put into this game. Three games a week means you recover, try to squeeze a couple of minutes out of a session to do tactical stuff to prepare for the opponent, do set-pieces and then go again. In this week it was completely different, we liked that and now we have another week like this and I am looking forward to it.'

Saturday, August 31st, 5.30pm
Premier League
Burnley 0, Liverpool 3

Goals: Wood (33og), Mane (37), Firmino (80)

Line-up (4-3-3): Adrian, Alexander-Arnold, Matip, Van Dijk, Robertson, Wijnaldum, Fabinho, Henderson (c) (Oxlade-Chamberlain 71), Salah, Firmino (Origi 85), Mane (Shaqiri 85). Subs not used: Kelleher, Milner, Gomez, Lallana

Jürgen's post-match reaction: 'It was pretty much the best second-ball game we've played since I have been together with the boys. We were really there, we won pretty much all of the first balls, which is difficult enough against Barnes and Wood. They have a good formation for the second balls. It was just amazing, [we were] using the space for immediate passing, trying to be quick in our decision-making. We scored a bit of a lucky goal but I think we still deserved to be 1-0 up. The second goal, brilliant. Just brilliant. Winning the ball, really quick decision-making and then a super pass from Bobby and a super finish from Sadio. The third goal, brilliant. There are so many different things and there is still space for improvement, which is cool.'

Post-match notes

This was the Reds' 13th consecutive league victory, a club record.

SEP

2019

The defence of Liverpool's European crown began with the toughest of assignments. Klopp would have to be at his canniest as he balanced cup commitments with fierce league tests. By the end of the month the Reds had confirmed their status as title contenders

14th: Newcastle United (PL) H
17th: SSC Napoli (CL) A
22nd: Chelsea (PL) A
25th: MK Dons (CC) A
28th: Sheffield United (PL) A

v Newcastle United
Saturday, September 14th, 12.30pm

'WE HAVE PROVED TIME AND AGAIN THAT FACTORS OUTSIDE OUR CONTROL WON'T AFFECT US IF WE DON'T LET THEM'

Premier League

September 2019

HELLO and welcome back to Anfield for our Premier League game against Newcastle United.

I'm sure none of us need reminding just how tough today's opponent is. It wasn't that long ago, right at the end of last season in fact, that we faced each other in the North East of England and – wow – what a contest that was.

I think of all the games we played last season, domestically and in Europe, that match up in Newcastle was one of the most fiercely-contested I can remember. They came at us with everything and that means we should expect the same today.

Of course there have been changes at Newcastle since, but from what I have seen early on they are just as strong and dangerous now.

I welcome Steve Bruce, his players, staff, officials and supporters of Newcastle to Anfield.

Steve's record as a manager in England is outstanding and I only have to listen to a number of my players who have worked with him to understand why he is held in such high regard.

Both Jordan Henderson and Andy Robertson speak with great affection of the help he gave them in developing and progressing during their careers. The stories they tell make it clear this is a manager whose players believe in him and will fight for him.

I expect this today.

I am not usually a person to point at individual results as an indicator for an opponent – analysis should include much, much more than this – but Newcastle's performance and result against Spurs in North London is definitely something to be aware of.

They were outstanding and proved as a team that they relish those sort of games. For a start their own home ground is a wonderful, passionate arena, so games like today are what they are all about. We must be ready.

Of course, we focus on ourselves – this will never change.

Ahead of the break we were in a very good moment. The performances against Arsenal and Burnley were of a high team and individual standard. But the international break does re-set the clock a little and therefore we must all be ready to switch back on.

Because of international call-ups we haven't had the majority of the squad together for long to prepare for this game. I know we are not unique and every team is affected. But it does impact.

What's important is that we stick to the values that have served us so well. Values of embracing hard work, doing the right things, being relentless, staying together and most importantly ensuring we bring the intensity in everything we do.

A break from being together might impact a little on preparation and therefore rhythm, although I would argue we have the mentality and character to combat this. But it does not and must not be allowed to impact on our intensity of approach. This is the same with it being an early kick-off. We have proved time and time again that factors outside our control won't affect us if we don't allow them.

The period coming between now and the next break for international football will be very busy for players and supporters alike. My players have the most outstanding attitude when it comes to recognising their responsibilities to the team and club during these moments.

They recognise contribution isn't just about who are the 11 names on a team sheet today. It's about making sure everyone is ready at all times to play their part, whatever that involves. It's about making sure training remains of the highest quality, whether it be short or long sessions.

We have set our own benchmarks and we can decide if we want to maintain and even surpass them. The opponents we face will be of the highest quality, but this is always the case at the level we compete at. I have zero doubt in this squad – they know what is required of them each and every day.

And the same applies to our amazing supporters. It feels like a long time ago we were all together at Anfield for a game, so I'm sure all will arrive here today with their 'game face' on.

I mentioned at the beginning about the game at Newcastle last season. A big part of that game was how ferocious their supporters were in backing their team. I'm pretty sure we expect the same in the away section this afternoon.

So, in the same way, the players need to increase their performance levels to take on this Newcastle, so must we all.

Liverpool 3, Newcastle United 1

Goals: Mane (28, 40), Salah (72)

Line-up (4-3-3): Adrian, Alexander-Arnold, Matip, Van Dijk (c), Robertson, Oxlade-Chamberlain (Milner 75), Fabinho, Wijnaldum (Shaqiri 84), Salah, Mane, Origi (Firmino 37). Subs not used: Kelleher, Gomez, Henderson, Lallana

Jürgen's post-match reaction: 'I started enjoying after 25 minutes around about when we arrived finally in the game. We needed another 15, 16 minutes [after Newcastle scored] to set the rhythm because you have to play much quicker than we did in the first part of the game. In the moment when we started doing that, immediately we had chances, scored two wonderful goals. Second half we scored only one goal, but we played really good football.'

Post-match notes

Sadio Mane became the first player in Premier League history to reach 50 home appearances with one club without defeat [41 wins, nine draws].

Tuesday, September 17th, 8pm
UEFA Champions League,
SSC Napoli 2, Liverpool 0

Line-up (4-3-3): Adrian, Alexander-Arnold, Matip, Van Dijk, Robertson, Fabinho, Milner (Wijnaldum 66), Henderson (c) (Shaqiri 87), Firmino, Mane, Salah. Subs not used: Kelleher, Lovren, Gomez, Oxlade-Chamberlain, Lallana

Jürgen's post-match reaction: 'It was much more of a game than last year when we played here and lost 1-0. We had a lot of good moments; I think we controlled the game in a lot of moments, we had a lot of interceptions, we won the ball and had counter-attacks. Both teams showed a lot of respect for each other, very compact, defended well and that's how you play a game against a strong side. It was really hard work for both teams. The second half was a bit [more with] wilder moments - counter-attack, counter-attack and then lose the ball when you are in the box and then have to run back. Then we started to control the game again and then we conceded the first goal and that was the game-changer tonight. We have to accept the result and we do that. We are really critical with ourselves but it was not a really, really bad performance; it was a game which you can win at Napoli, but we didn't because we didn't score. You want to then have at least a point and we didn't get that because of the penalty [scored by Dries Mertens after 82 minutes].'

Sunday, September 22nd, 4.30pm
Premier League
Chelsea 1, Liverpool 2

Goals: Alexander-Arnold (14), Firmino (30)

Line-up (4-3-3): Adrian, Alexander-Arnold, Matip, Van Dijk, Robertson, Wijnaldum, Fabinho, Henderson (c) (Lallana 84), Salah (Gomez 90+2), Firmino, Mane (Milner 71). Subs not used: Kelleher, Oxlade-Chamberlain, Shaqiri, Brewster

Jürgen's post-match reaction: 'I think I shouldn't be surprised any more about the character of my team, to be honest. We don't tell [ourselves] every day, 'Oh my God, your character is brilliant, your character is outstanding, you have the best character of all of the characters!' It is not like this. We expect it from ourselves that we fight for everything. We have a big job to do in a really difficult league. Everybody thinks we should be first or second – but we have to play the football for it. We don't think about these things, we just have to play to try to win football games. That's what we did. Yes, without character life is difficult, but football is impossible. I was not in doubt about that. The boys did really well, they fought really hard and yes, all good. I don't think there is any other way to win here. It is a difficult place to come, it is a while ago we won here, so it feels big, to be honest. It's a big one. We have to be ready every day, every matchday and that's what the boys were.'

Wednesday, September 25th, 7.45pm
Carabao Cup third round
MK Dons 0, Liverpool 2

Goals: Milner (41), Hoever (69)

Line-up (4-3-3): Kelleher, Hoever (Van den Berg 90+2), Gomez, Lovren, Milner (c), Jones, Keita (Chirivella 63), Lallana, Oxlade-Chamberlain (Kane 82), Brewster, Elliott. Subs not used: Lonergan, Lewis, Longstaff, Clarkson

Jürgen's post-match reaction: 'It's so important that we are brave enough to use the boys. We are not here with this line-up because we don't respect the competition, we are here to win the game. We don't fly to London with all that stuff and then say goodbye. So I am really happy that we went through, that's cool and that the boys felt adult football as well, that's really important. Very physical situations for offensive players especially. But still they could show in moments how good they are, so it's a big step for them and I am really happy. We believe in them but they have to make the next steps. I told them after the game, the last 10 minutes, these boys are naturally fit but you saw it was not the game any more. They lost it and that's not okay. Then you see Millie running around. Whatever I tell them is not the same as if they see it on the pitch. This man [Milner] is on fire. It helps a lot. He's a role model for young players. If he could play every day, Millie would be like this every day. Absolutely brilliant.'

Saturday, September 28th, 12.30pm
Premier League
Sheffield United 0, Liverpool 1

Goal: Wijnaldum (70)

Line-up (4-3-3): Adrian, Alexander-Arnold, Matip, Van Dijk, Robertson, Henderson (c) (Origi 64), Fabinho, Wijnaldum, Salah, Firmino (Milner 87), Mane (Oxlade-Chamberlain 90+4). Subs not used: Kelleher, Lovren, Gomez, Lallana

Jürgen's post-match reaction: 'Eight times 1-0 is more important than one time 8-0. If you give me the guarantee for it, I would take the next eight games [as 1-0 wins] but it is difficult. We are very critical of ourselves, but it is not the moment for being critical – you just have to respect the effort we put in because that was exactly what we had to do. We fought. As I said before the game, is it allowed that Sheffield United fight more than us? No. And they didn't. Did they run more? No. That was important and then if you do that, then you can have the chance to deserve the three points. Very often around goals, you can have a little bit of luck – but this time it looks like we needed a lot of luck. I am completely fine with it. I don't think we had an 'off day' because today it was much more important that we are really ready to fight than ready to play our best football because your best football you play in moments, but fighting you do for the whole 95 minutes. That's what we did and that's how we deserved it.'

OCT

2019

Klopp's men played six games in the month of October and failed to keep a clean sheet in any of them...so it's a good job the goalscoring machine was in full effect as the Reds averaged three goals per match. Still unbeaten at the end of October, it was clear the boss had his team primed for a title race

2nd: FC Salzburg (CL) H
5th: Leicester City (PL) H
20th: Manchester United (PL) A
23rd: KRC Genk (CL) A
27th: Tottenham Hotspur (PL) H
30th: Arsenal (CC) H

v FC Salzburg
Wednesday, October 2nd, 8pm

'RESILIENCE AND FIGHTING FOR A WIN ISN'T A DIFFERENT SIDE TO US – IT'S AT OUR CORE'

UEFA Champions League

October 2019

GOOD evening and welcome back to Anfield for our UEFA Champions League game against FC Salzburg.

I cannot tell you how delighted I am to be back at our home this evening – I love this place.

Our games on the road haven't been too bad in truth. Fantastic and hard-fought wins against Chelsea, MK Dons and Sheffield United. I won't ignore the result against Napoli and because of the competition we play tonight it is relevant. But even in Napoli we played a very good game, but the outcome was not what we hoped for and quite honestly wasn't what we deserved.

But despite three successive wins away, we couldn't be more full of joy to be back on the Anfield pitch and playing in this amazing place, in front of our wonderful supporters.

I'm writing this column before performing any of the pre-match press duties, but I suspect there will be a lot of focus on the amazing European nights we experienced at Anfield the previous season, probably most notably the last one here.

I have no problem talking or thinking about the amazing nights we have already had, but I'm much more interested in creating a situation where we can enjoy more like it. This team is much more concerned with 'the next one' than 'the last one'. This is how we have to be.

In our situation, looking back is only useful if we take

the information and experiences from it that help us. If we look back – as a collective – and remember that by making Anfield a cauldron of noise and positivity, we help affect performance in the best way possible, I'm good with that.

Of course, as always, responsibility lies with us to perform in a way that inspires. But I keep using the word 'love' about being back at home tonight and I'm repeating it because it's the overriding feeling.

I love that this is our home and we make it unique. I love that we have our own way. Our own atmosphere. I know we will need it tonight and we will need it as much as any European game we have played in this place in the past four years.

I welcome Jesse Marsch, his players, staff, officials and supporters of FC Salzburg to Liverpool. For the visiting fans, I hope they get a chance to enjoy the hospitality and warmth of this wonderful city.

What an incredible team and a superb head-coach they have. Jesse has them in a really good way.

They are so positive and their results show this. They love to attack and they are a team that attacks with confidence and scores often. Their opening result in the group saw them score six against Genk. Trust me when I tell you that this says more about the quality of Salzburg than it does the weakness of Genk.

This weekend, another four goals in a domestic game.

Really good side. Excellent players. Great leadership. Tough, tough opponent. Really tough.

But this is the Champions League and you don't face anyone who isn't of the highest quality. It's why it's such an amazing competition.

And what's really cool is that we are a good side also, with plenty of quality. I don't think I need to talk too much about this – we have seen it from this incredible group of players time and time again. So, I trust that even though we take on a very difficult team, we do so respecting them but focusing on our own strengths, our own qualities.

There was a lot of focus after Sheffield United about us showing a different side of ourselves to win. I struggle to accept that notion. I don't see resilience and fighting for a win as being a different side to us – it's at our core.

The will to win, the determination to get a result, that's always been our central ambition. There are some games that appear more fluid or maybe appear more complete. But the desire to give all you have and fight in every second in a fair and competitive way is us. It's brought us to where we are as a team in this moment.

Returning to the point I made at the very beginning, we are back at home tonight after what feels like an extended time away from Anfield, but I'm certain it won't take us long to feel like we've never been away.

Our visitors from Austria will make loud noise constantly. Sadio and Naby have both spoken to me about how passionate their supporters are and told the boys they create a really inspiring atmosphere for their players. This is cool because I know in these moments Anfield responds with its best face.

It's a Champions League game, under the lights, and the result is really important and significant. So there is a job to do for all of us.

Let's do it!

Liverpool 4, Salzburg 3

Goals: Mane (9), Robertson (25), Salah (36, 69)

Line-up (4-3-3): Adrian, Alexander-Arnold, Gomez, Van Dijk, Robertson, Henderson (c) (Milner 62), Fabinho, Wijnaldum (Origi 64), Salah (Keita 90+1), Firmino, Mane. Subs not used: Kelleher, Lovren, Oxlade-Chamberlain, Lallana

Jürgen's post-match reaction: 'There are teams that would maybe break down after 3-0 at Anfield – but they were not really bothered. We opened the door and they were running through, chasing through the door. They scored their goal, then at half-time we tried to adjust but all the goals they scored – first goal, we lost the ball easy; second or third goal, we lost the ball easy. Counter-attacks when you are 3-1 up makes not a lot of sense. It was a very important lesson for us tonight, but I prefer massively to learn it in the game than after the game because if we would have lost 4-3 it would have been the same lesson.'

v Leicester City
Saturday, October 5th, 3pm

'THE QUALITY OF TEAM BRENDAN LEFT FOR ME WAS A FANTASTIC LEGACY FOR ANY MANAGER'

Premier League

GOOD afternoon and welcome back to Anfield for the Premier League game against Leicester City.

We had to wait what felt like an eternity for a home game and now we have one so soon after a hectic Champions League contest on Wednesday.

I don't really want to go over that game too much, other than to say for long periods we played some unbelievable football and in others, not so cool. But as I said after, every game can be a lesson and I would rather learn things while winning games.

Credit to the team, because of Community Shield and UEFA Super Cup we have had one of the more challenging starts to the season, but when questions are asked of these players they find answers.

I noticed on Wednesday that Christian Fuchs was here doing Austrian TV and I'm sure he will have taken back some information for our visitors today. Unfortunately for us the rest of the Leicester side were feet up and resting while we were playing, so the opponent we face today will be fresh as well as full of confidence.

I welcome Brendan Rodgers, his players, staff, officials and supporters of Leicester to Anfield today.

For Brendan – what can I say, other than welcome back to a good friend of this club.

It can be strange when you follow a manager into a club, because in recognising the excellent work they have done you are almost questioning why they have left in the first place. Of course, these are not decisions we make as coaches or managers ourselves.

Here's what I do know: I was very fortunate to inherit the team I did from Brendan. I watched from Germany and admired greatly what he did at Liverpool in his time here. He built a team with a clear identity and purpose. A team who were adventurous and clever. And it was a team who enjoyed success.

I can honestly say, hand-on-heart, the quality of team Brendan left and the good shape they were in was a fantastic legacy for any manager.

The beneficiaries of Brendan's guidance now are Leicester City and what a start to the season they have enjoyed. Again, great performances and brilliant results. So hard to play against, so difficult to stop what they do. Be it home or away, they are a constant threat.

I honestly can't think of a tougher opponent to face in this moment at Anfield and I know they will be very motivated. They've always done well against us since I've been here and now they are again on the upward trajectory.

Aside from Brendan returning, it will also be great to see Kolo Toure again. What a guy! We didn't work together that long but in the time we did, he gave me and the team absolutely everything.

I'm sure the sort of personality Kolo is, he will be learning all he can from Brendan before being ready to lead a club himself in the future. Both Brendan and Kolo, plus other members of his staff, will, I'm sure, be given a warm welcome back. Although for the game itself we press 'pause' on the friendship button.

Turning back to ourselves, today is the final game in this mini-block of fixtures before another break. I have run out of words to praise the squad for their commitment.

This is a period where getting over the line in games is important. It is not always possible to have the best rhythm every time we play. Some teams do have it – Leicester being a perfect example. We, in this moment, are playing in a very smart way I think. We have periods of games we play football not to be rivalled, and other times we have to show clever game-management. I am absolutely fine with this.

Also, as is always the case, the importance of the whole squad has never been more visible, in training and in the games. I have no idea which 11 will start today at the time of writing this column, but I know I can rely on every player on our roster if and when called upon.

The game on Wednesday proved that even if you don't start, coming on is just as important to impact the result. What is key is you must be ready. It is the one expectation I have and, in fairness, these boys always deliver.

Finally, the atmosphere at Anfield on Wednesday was again sensational – but as with the team, we will require another big push today. I don't want to over-state this, having mentioned repeatedly, but Leicester are in a good moment. Their fans, like their team, will come here with a feeling of positivity.

But we need no reminder of our responsibilities because it's our stadium, our pitch, our home, our Anfield. We can make it special again and I'm sure we will – by going again and giving our all together.

Liverpool 2, Leicester City 1

Goals: Mane (40), Milner (90+5pen)

Line-up (4-3-3): Adrian, Alexander-Arnold, Lovren, Van Dijk, Robertson, Wijnaldum (Henderson 78), Fabinho, Milner (c), Salah (Lallana 90+2), Mane, Firmino (Origi 78). Subs not used: Kelleher, Keita, Gomez, Elliott

Jürgen's post-match reaction: 'We are not fussed by the situation where people talk to us about the winning streak or whatever. They didn't look a second like a team who won so many games that they don't have the desire any more to win another one. It looked like they had never won a game before, and I love that fact. The stadium atmosphere was brilliant, 1-1 and everything was positive in the stadium, that's just so helpful. It was all over a really good performance by the whole Liverpool family. But now the boys travel all over the world and hopefully they come back healthy and then we prepare [for] Manchester United.'

Sunday, October 20th, 4.30pm
Premier League
Manchester United 1, Liverpool 1

Goal: Lallana (85)

Line-up (4-3-3): Alisson, Alexander-Arnold, Matip, Van Dijk, Robertson, Wijnaldum (Keita 82), Fabinho, Henderson (c) (Lallana 71), Origi (Oxlade-Chamberlain 60), Firmino, Mane. Subs not used: Adrian, Lovren, Gomez, Milner

Jürgen's post-match reaction: 'We were not at all unpredictable, when we could have turned the other way around because we were not orientated, like kind of impressed with the challenges they made, we didn't play real football. But then with just Hendo a bit higher we had then immediately the ball and then first the two guys in between the lines, which helped massively and caused them problems. We didn't have chance after chance, but we deserved that goal, I think we are all agreed about that. Then Naby was on, helped as well, fresh legs, being there, passing safe and then not always doing the obvious things, moving higher and passing the ball and that's how the goal happened. We can pass the ball to Robbo and he has to run sideways and not make the ball or you can pass it exactly in that way and he can make the cross so that we can score the goal. We were better with the three boys coming on, that helped a lot and I'm happy about that of course, especially about the fact that Adam scored this goal.'

Wednesday, October 23rd, 8pm UEFA Champions League, KRC Genk 1, Liverpool 4

Goals: Oxlade-Chamberlain (2, 57), Mane (77), Salah (87)

Line-up (4-3-3): Alisson, Milner (c), Lovren, Van Dijk, Robertson (Gomez 63), Oxlade-Chamberlain (Wijnaldum 74), Fabinho, Keita, Salah, Firmino (Origi 80), Mane. Subs not used: Adrian, Henderson, Lallana, Brewster

Jürgen's post-match reaction: 'They started with a 4-4-2 so it was for a midfield press, we have to play around. We were really flexible, we did that well. We didn't create too much but it was exactly [right]: keep them busy, find the gaps, pass it through, pass it behind, all that stuff. That was the plan obviously, and it worked for 10 or 15 minutes and then not any more because we lost unexpected balls, which we were not ready for, which in the formation is not possible because if you are in a wide formation and lose the ball in the centre… we lost too many of them and sometimes we took in the wrong moment a risk. Then we scored the second goal, the first goal was brilliant but the second was even nicer – all our goals were unbelievably beautiful – and the second was like it was a proper knock for Genk it looked like. So we scored a third and fourth and then conceded one, which is not cool, but it's not for us the biggest problem in the world. We won the game, job done, that's it.'

v Tottenham Hotspur
Sunday, October 27th, 4.30pm

'BE READY TO RESPOND TO SETBACKS. BE READY. BE SMART. PLAY YOUR FOOTBALL'

Premier League

October 2019

GOOD afternoon and welcome back to Anfield for our Premier League encounter against Tottenham Hotspur.

Both sides come into this game on the back of Champions League midweek matches and wins. That in itself tells us the quality and danger we face today. One of England and Europe's top clubs, is here on Merseyside, hungry for points. We must be ready to fight with all we have.

We know from experience how tough an opponent Red Star Belgrade are, because of our battles against them last season. The confidence and belief Tottenham showed in comprehensively beating them should silence anyone foolish enough to think they have dropped off at all.

Anyone with an ounce of knowledge of their side knows they are even stronger than last term. They have added quality to their ranks and kept their key players again. And they have their world-class leader in the dugout.

I welcome Mauricio Pochettino, his players, staff, officials and supporters of Tottenham to Anfield.

My admiration for Mauricio is well-known and I, as much as anyone, can associate with the challenges he faces at this moment, after such a thrilling campaign last season when his team enjoyed an incredible ride. It is a job to do to pick up and go again – but do it you must.

The truth about his management is that he always improves teams. His sides progress. They get better season on season. I look at Spurs now and I know they have all the tools to be right in the conversation for trophies domestically and in Europe over the next eight months or so.

The games in which we faced each other last season were all so incredibly close – fine margins. I would expect the same again in the matches we play this time.

It is about being concentrated at all times. Be individually and collectively at your best. Be ready to respond to setbacks. Be brave. Be smart. Play your football. When two really good sides face each other, these are the factors that decide it.

I mention Tottenham's excellent midweek win and of course we also had a good night on the Wednesday. Spurs have had the extra day's rest and were at home, but I don't see playing Sunday-Wednesday-Sunday as an issue, so no excuses our end.

In our last two fixtures we have shown many qualities. At Manchester United we didn't show our very best face, but under difficult circumstances we found a way and that in itself is an encouragement.

We took control of the game and I feel the same now as I did at the time, and that is if one team deserved to win, it was us.

In Genk we played some really nice football and the

result is important for the group and our chances of qualification. We 'park' that competition now as we have domestic games, starting today against Tottenham, before playing Arsenal at Anfield midweek and then Aston Villa away.

There were some nice stories from our last couple of games and they highlight perfectly the importance of the squad and contribution.

We were all so pleased for Adam Lallana in Manchester because this player deserved this moment so much. My opposition manager knows Adam's personal and professional qualities as well as I do, but he's had to be patient for a while now and I can imagine with his quality that is not easy. Such a top player, strong and fit, in a great moment. Opportunities haven't been what he deserves until now but he took his one at Old Trafford, performance-wise, so well.

Naby Keita and Joe Gomez demonstrated why they are big figures for us with their efforts in Genk. Naby was great coming on, even though late, at Old Trafford and then was brilliant in Belgium.

For Joe, the attitude and intensity he showed when coming on on Wednesday is just what he and we need. Outstanding from him and we will need him a lot.

Finally: the Ox. He's been close to those sort of moments this season, and again, like a few players, I'm sure he craves as many minutes on the pitch as possible.

But in our team it's about being ready and taking your chance. Ox has been fantastic and those truly wonderful goals were great reward.

I'm sure the atmosphere will be big at Anfield today because it's a big, big game. We will need the crowd to be the wind at our back. I think games like this – with two great teams and clubs – deserve special energy in the ground and I know we will get it. Hopefully we can reward our fans with a contest to enjoy.

Liverpool 2, Tottenham Hotspur 1

Goals: Henderson (52), Salah (75pen)

Line-up (4-3-3): Alisson, Alexander-Arnold, Lovren, Van Dijk, Robertson, Henderson (c), Fabinho, Wijnaldum (Milner 77), Salah (Gomez 85), Firmino (Origi 90+3), Mane. Subs not used: Adrian, Keita, Oxlade-Chamberlain, Lallana

Jürgen's post-match reaction: 'I am absolutely pleased, but to be honest I expect it as well. An early goal is obviously not the best thing that can happen, but sometimes it makes one thing clear: game on. That's exactly what we expected Tottenham to do, being very compact, being very aggressive, chasing us. It was a bit unlucky for us because Ali made first a save and then Harry [Kane] was there. So, I am pleased, but I expect it as well. The game I loved, a super game. It was just how football should look, how you should play against a really strong, good, organised side with the threat constantly in your mind that each ball you lose will possibly end up in front of your own goal.'

October 2019

v Arsenal
Wednesday, October 30th, 7.30pm

'WE DON'T HAVE FIRST AND SECOND CHOICES – WE HAVE A TEAM FOR A PARTICULAR MOMENT'

Carabao Cup fourth round

GOOD evening and welcome back to Anfield for our Carabao Cup tie against Arsenal. I welcome Unai Emery, his players, staff, officials and supporters of the Gunners back to Liverpool for their second visit this season.

Because our encounter wasn't too long ago, I don't want to be overly repetitive with things I say, except my admiration for him as a coach remains of the absolute highest regard. A coach who has already won big trophies in both Spain and France. Someone who is a winner. Whose teams play with tenacity and guile. His team is packed with adventure and players whose natural-born instincts are to attack.

Clearly, calling the line-up this evening might be a little more complicated, but whatever side Unai selects it will be full of positive intent and we must be ready and we must be on our toes at all times, or we will be punished.

There is much to admire about this Arsenal team – both in terms of what they have done last season and the progress they make this.

For us – also speaking candidly on line-up – as I write this column I really cannot give an indication of who will start and who will not.

I'm sure, because of our schedule and because of the side we picked against MK Dons, there'll be assumptions of changes. It's a fair assumption, but what is absolutely not okay is to indicate that it shows a lessening of our intent in this competition.

I love the words of Pep Lijnders when he says we don't have anything but first-choice players in this squad and he is so right. We don't have first and second choices – really we don't. We have the team for a particular moment.

Tonight we select a team to win. Winning is our first, second and third motivation – the only motivation always.

Although not certain, the strong likelihood is that a number of our younger players will feature in some capacity tonight.

In Milton Keynes, Caoimhin Kelleher, Ki-Jana Hoever, Curtis Jones, Harvey Elliott and Rhian Brewster all started and equipped themselves superbly. Herbie Kane, Pedro Chirivella and Sepp van den Berg all came on from the bench. Ki-Jana isn't available to us at the moment because he is away with the Dutch national team with his respective age-group.

The attitude these players showed in the last round is exactly what will be required this evening, if again given the opportunity.

They show the right attitude and the perfect amount of hunger each and every day they train with us at Melwood. They show us, in their actions, that they understand what an immense privilege it is to represent a club like Liverpool – it's an honour all of us blessed to work here feel.

Clearly the ability of these players is not in question. It is their talent that has brought them here and kept them here. At this stage of their careers it is about a variety of other factors – and being ready to grasp an opportunity is a big part of it.

It is appropriate to point to Trent Alexander-Arnold when discussing this. This month three years ago he made his first-team debut. Against Tottenham at the weekend he made his 99th appearance for the senior side.

The reason he has achieved this in such a short space of time, one of the four youngest in LFC history I believe, isn't just because he has amazing ability. It is because of how he has handled himself, taken his chances and dealt with setbacks and difficulties.

There won't be a player in our current first-team squad who hasn't faced these challenges at a young age. It is the job of all of us to help them and nurture them and give them an environment to grow, develop and flourish. I am confident we are doing this.

And on that theme, again on the assumption there are some Anfield debuts for our young players this evening, it is critical that the atmosphere is one that encourages and inspires. I know our crowd will get this – they are world class when it comes to recognising their job also.

Arsenal will have the highest motivation. Anfield will need to be an energy source as it was at the weekend, when it kept the team driving forward.

Hopefully we can all play our part in making tonight a memorable one for the LFC family for all the right reasons.

Liverpool 5, Arsenal 5 (after extra time, Liverpool win 5-4 on penalties)

Goals: Mustafi (6og), Milner (43pen), Oxlade-Chamberlain (58), Origi (62, 90+4)

Line-up (4-3-3): Kelleher, Williams, Gomez, Van den Berg, Milner (c), Oxlade-Chamberlain (Chirivella 81), Lallana, Keita (Jones 55), Elliott, Brewster, Origi. Subs not used: Adrian, Kane, Larouci, Clarkson, Koumetio

Jürgen's post-match reaction: 'Everybody who came tonight to Anfield saw 19 goals, which is pretty special. Really perfect, absolutely perfect. You need to be born in Liverpool probably to do that [on Curtis Jones stepping up to take the winning penalty]. It was not my idea. When I saw the list the last time, Divock was on five and Curtis on four. When I saw the number four coming and it was Divock then I thought, 'Okay, obviously they changed it'. Good situation. Curtis has no issue with self-confidence, he absolutely doesn't struggle in that department. It's good. It's absolutely nice. I'm really pleased for him, like I am pleased for Caoimhin saving that penalty, pleased for Neco, who played an incredible game and giving the assist to Div's goal.'

NOV

2019

This was showing all the signs of being a special season. Klopp had a job keeping everyone's feet on the ground as the Reds powered to an eight-point lead in the table. The fact they had beaten the reigning champions made dampening that enthusiasm even more difficult...

2nd: Aston Villa (PL) A
5th: KRC Genk (CL) H
10th: Manchester City (PL) H
23rd: Crystal Palace (PL) A
27th: SSC Napoli (CL) H
30th: Brighton (PL) H

Saturday, November 2nd, 3pm
Premier League
Aston Villa 1, Liverpool 2

Goals: Robertson (87), Mane (90+4)

Line-up (4-3-3): Alisson, Alexander-Arnold, Lovren, Van Dijk, Robertson, Lallana (Keita 84), Henderson (c), Wijnaldum (Oxlade-Chamberlain 65), Salah (Origi 65), Firmino, Mane. Subs not used: Adrian, Gomez, Fabinho, Milner

Jürgen's post-match reaction: 'That was really satisfying. The routine [for Mane's goal], we'd tried before a couple of times and we thought it could be a space where we could make a little advantage. It was not the only routine we had, but it was one I saw in the game two or three times before. We worked yesterday on that and then if you can use it in a very decisive moment then it's really good. Sadio [also] crossed the ball for Robbo's goal. Being there for that goal after the situations he had in the game when he got a yellow card – I think when you see it back, it is for sure not diving, there is contact, but it is the decision you have to accept. In the moment, then the crowd takes you a little and try to make you even more insecure – but that's obviously not possible with Sadio. He stayed in the game, got the yellow card, but still stayed in the game, even defensively. Very good. It is lucky when you score these goals but I think if you watch the game, then I think if one team deserved to win it then it is us.'

v KRC Genk
Tuesday, November 5th, 8pm

'A CHAMPIONS LEAGUE GAME IS A HEAVYWEIGHT WORLD TITLE FIGHT EVERY TIME'

UEFA Champions League

GOOD evening and welcome back to Anfield for our UEFA Champions League group game against KRC Genk.

It wasn't that long ago that we met over in Belgium. Because of how the group draw is made, it so happens that we play each other back-to-back in this competition. I don't think this has the biggest influence, other than maybe our knowledge of each other is a little fresher than it otherwise would be.

The match in Genk brought a win for us, but we saw on that night what a threat they pose. They had a lot of chances and gave us a lot of problems we had to solve. The goals we scored on the night were of the highest quality, so this tells us we needed to be at our very best to secure the win.

In the Champions League so far their performances have been very good. Their first game against Red Bull Salzburg – wow – I don't think I have ever seen a game where the scoreline and the level of performance were so far apart. Genk did not deserve the final result they got that night, they deserved so much better. And then they proved how good they can be at this level with a fantastic draw against Napoli.

We know from personal experience the quality and ability of Napoli, so the result they got against them says everything. And as I have already said, even in the defeat to us, they can take a lot of credit.

I welcome Felice Mazzù, his players, staff, officials and of course the visiting supporters of Genk to Anfield.

Felice is undoubtedly one of the most progressive managerial talents in Belgium and his achievements at Genk speak for themselves. They were inventive in how they set up against us in Belgium and I would suspect they have a plan for us again this evening.

I think we must prepare for a team that will come and embrace everything that is truly magical about this competition and that involves playing teams like us at Anfield. What I see in their approach is that they will take extra energy from the occasion and it will lift them. This makes them more dangerous for us. We must be ready for them.

For the Genk travelling supporters, I really hope they get a chance to enjoy the amazing city of Liverpool. In the ground I am expecting the same level of noise that we experienced in Belgium. They never stopped supporting their team and I admire this so much.

Also, what incredible class they showed with their appreciation for Divock Origi. This is how football and life should be – total commitment for your own team but also respect and appreciation for returning friends. I know it will have meant a lot to Divock.

Turning to us specifically, there is work for us to do tonight and we cannot and must not have our focus anywhere but here. We must be in the moment.

We saw just how tight the group was last season. The very last kick of the very last group game could have put us out. If you, for even half-a-second, lose sight of how hard this competition is and how precious each and every point is, trust me, we will not have the experiences like we enjoyed the last couple of seasons.

A Champions League game, be it group or knockout, is a heavyweight world title fight every time. Every team you face has the quality to beat you and to knock you to the canvas. These teams don't just have a puncher's chance, they are winners with a winner's approach.

If you have the wrong attitude or the wrong mindset you will lose. There is no question of this.

I'm not particularly interested what happens elsewhere in the other groups but I am pretty sure it is the same in all of them. The final answer for group standings will almost certainly go to the last game again.

I have no worries about our approach tonight because I know this team and this club is streetwise enough to know what is needed. We have that institutional knowledge ingrained in us that a Champions League night, be it at Anfield or away, is an occasion to relish and respect. As a club we don't take these nights for granted and that must show in our performance.

And by 'our performance' I mean all of us. Players, management, staff and supporters. We all come here and show our best face. Genk absolutely will – so if we don't, we risk our future in a competition we are in love with. If last season taught us anything it is that the European Cup isn't just won on the night of the final. It is won in every minute you play in the tournament.

Finally, I would like to thank our remarkable supporters for the last two games, both of which finished in quite dramatic fashion. Before the Carabao Cup game I asked that we show the team that's selected what a proper Anfield night feels like and we got that in abundance. At Aston Villa the energy from the away end was a huge factor in us keeping belief that we could do it, right until the very end.

This evening I think the role of the supporters in helping the team set the right tone is essential. If we all show the same hunger for the three group points, I think we can have another Anfield evening to enjoy.

Liverpool 2, KRC Genk 1

Goals: Wijnaldum (14), Oxlade-Chamberlain (53)

Line-up (4-3-3): Alisson, Alexander-Arnold, Gomez, Van Dijk, Milner (c), Wijnaldum, Fabinho, Keita (Robertson 74), Salah, Oxlade-Chamberlain (Mane 75), Origi (Firmino 89). Subs not used: Adrian, Lovren, Lallana, Jones

Jürgen's post-match reaction: "Job done' is the headline from the game, pretty much. But the group is not decided. We knew from the beginning it's a tough group. Yes, now we are first in the table but we only really want to be first after the last matchday.'

v Manchester City
Sunday, November 10th, 4.30pm

'IT'S A GAME BETWEEN TWO EXCEPTIONAL SETS OF PLAYERS, THAT MATTERS A GREAT DEAL'

Premier League

GOOD afternoon and welcome back to Anfield for our Premier League contest against Manchester City.

Well, I think it's fair to say a match like this needs no additional hype. What an occasion we have to look forward to, and one where we should all embrace the joy and positivity of it.

Our opponent today is one of, if not the best team in the world. We have proved in recent seasons we are not too bad also, so can legitimately expect to be in a similar conversation.

I'm sure by the time kick-off comes around there will have been many words said and many issues inflated to make this feel like more than a football match. But, you know what, it is just that.

Nothing is decided today, not even close to it. There is enough to enjoy about this without turning it into something it's not.

It's an amazing fixture for sure, but after today is done there are 26 more to come in the Premier League this season I think? This means 78 points up for grabs still? So come on, let's enjoy this as a special match. Important yes, but far from decisive.

It's a game between two exceptional sets of players, that to both clubs and supporters matters a great deal – but it's a sporting contest and as such should be something that brings out the best qualities in all of us.

You don't have to flick too far on your TV or look

on the internet or in newspapers to see that in the UK, Europe and the wider world there are a lot of not-very-cool situations in this moment.

Football, even at our level where the so-called pressure and focus is very intense, is an opportunity for those involved to appreciate how fortunate we are and take joy from the moment.

What is there not to enjoy about this contest today? Both teams packed with creative, inventive, passionate, adventurous players who will give all they have for each other and the fans.

I welcome Pep Guardiola, his players, staff, officials and supporters of Manchester City to Anfield.

We have, of course, already met once this season, in the Community Shield at Wembley. What a game that was by the way – wow – the highest quality, energy and commitment for what was supposedly a 'curtain-raiser'. I think we saw there – and will no doubt see again today – that games between us always matter and are played with the highest intensity at all times.

The intensity of performance, from both sides, comes I think because of the respect we have for each other – across the spectrum.

I don't want to become repetitive with things I say about Pep in these columns. I've said time and time again I think he is the best manager in the world. That hasn't changed since I last said it. I could not hold him or his achievements in any higher regard, and that of his players also.

Their level of performance against us, in the games we play, is always so so high. I think it's the quality of these games and the willingness of both sides to give their everything that shows the esteem we hold each other in.

I have been asked in the build-up to today, and previous games like this, whether as a manager I enjoy them. Honestly speaking, I don't enjoy the 90-plus minutes itself when it's happening, but that's the case with nearly all games I've been involved with as a manager in my career.

When you're in the moment you are working, you don't allow yourself time to even think about whether it's something you enjoy or not. But I can enjoy the situation and I do.

I take enjoyment and fulfilment from how my players have improved and grown together to bring us to the point that we are involved in great occasions like this. I take enjoyment from the fact these players and this team have earned their status as being one of the best football sides in the world in this moment. I take enjoyment from knowing that these players have total belief in themselves.

I could not be prouder of what this squad has done and continues to do. Liverpool Football Club is so blessed to have this remarkable group of people together in this moment representing and competing for the club. They are so special, each and every one of them.

We cannot, and should not, ever promise an outcome. We can't promise a specific result today or that in May we will achieve anything specific either – that would be foolish.

What we can promise, and what they constantly deliver on, is that this team, whichever players feature on the team sheet today, will give their all. These players don't know any other way – it's all of themselves and nothing less when they compete for Liverpool.

Finally I normally finish this column by talking about our incredible supporters and I know they understand the critical importance of the positive energy they can bring us today. But there are a couple of people in the ground today I want to make a special mention of: Seán Cox and his incredible family.

Seán's story has touched all of us, and although initially the emotions were ones of sadness that his life has been so affected purely by coming to support the football team he loves, we now have new feelings when we hear his name mentioned.

Seán's name and that of his wife Martina and his wider family makes me think of courage, spirit and renewal.

Seán is an inspirational figure in this club's story now.

To know he plans to come back to Anfield – to support this club once more – brings perspective to so many things, both in football and life.

I hope all of us here today, whatever colours we wear, do him proud in how we approach this occasion.

Liverpool 3, Manchester City 1

Goals: Fabinho (6), Salah (13), Mane (51)

Line-up (4-3-3): Alisson, Alexander-Arnold, Lovren, Van Dijk, Robertson, Henderson (c) (Milner 61), Fabinho, Wijnaldum, Salah (Gomez 87), Firmino (Oxlade-Chamberlain 79), Mane. Subs not used: Adrian, Keita, Lallana, Origi

Jürgen's post-match reaction: 'I love the atmosphere, it was incredible, people just amazing, against an outstandingly strong opponent. Everybody asked me about – and I didn't see it yet – the penalty situation or handball before Fabinho scores. What I heard was handball from Bernardo Silva, but I can imagine it's not a situation Pep is really pleased with. I heard that 22 seconds later we were in front of their goal and Fabinho with his stunner brings us the 1-0 lead. The second goal we scored, I don't think I ever saw a goal like this. A right full-back with a 60-yard pass to the left full-back; two more touches and a cross over 40 yards, 50, and a header. That's pretty special. It was a good moment to score a goal like this. And the third goal very, very good as well, a sensational cross and Sadio in the right position. All around these three goals it was hardest work, and so the boys deserved these three points. Great.'

Saturday, November 23rd, 3pm
Premier League
Crystal Palace 1, Liverpool 2

Goals: Mane (49), Firmino (85)

Line-up (4-3-3): Alisson, Alexander-Arnold, Lovren, Van Dijk, Robertson, Henderson (c) (Milner 79), Fabinho, Wijnaldum, Oxlade-Chamberlain (Origi 64), Firmino (Gomez 89), Mane. Subs not used: Adrian, Keita, Lallana, Salah

Jürgen's post-match reaction: 'I'm not surprised at all that it was tough, to be honest. You probably saw all my games [against Palace] since I'm in England, they were always similar! We just know it's a tough place – the atmosphere is good, they don't give up. Crystal Palace doesn't need a lot of situations to stay in the game. The start was good. After that we always had good football moments, really good football, crisp passes as well. They were more often direct and did that pretty well, had moments after set-pieces. They [the players] come back from so many different national teams. So today I have absolutely no problem that we were not brilliant because in a game like this you just have to make sure that you fight for the right result. We did that from the first minute. Could we have played better? Yes, but we had players on the pitch that were on Thursday morning still in a plane back from Abu Dhabi, so that's not too cool. Getting a result at Crystal Palace is something we never take for granted.'

v SSC Napoli
Wednesday, November 27th, 8pm

'CARLO LEFT ME LOST FOR WORDS. THIS IS A VERY RARE OCCURRENCE!'

UEFA Champions League

GOOD evening and welcome back to Anfield for our UEFA Champions League game against SSC Napoli.

First of all I would like to extend a warm welcome to Carlo Ancelotti – quite simply one of the best people I know in the game.

Tonight is the third time we meet this season, although only the second in a competitive match. We played Napoli in Edinburgh pre-season and I think it's fair to say they got the better of the game that day.

However, my positive memory of the occasion in Scotland was the incredibly classy gesture from Carlo. He bought a very lovely bottle of red wine and wrote a touching congratulations message on it, for what we had achieved the season before.

I was suitably embarrassed in the moment he gave it to me, to the point I was lost for words. People who know me well will tell you this is a very rare occurrence.

Carlo is one of the all-time greats. His achievements as a player, coach and manager would take up the entirety of this programme if I was to list them. And achieved in different countries. Wow – so hard to do.

I have a confession to make to Carlo and that is that I still haven't drunk the wine. It takes pride of place at home. I'm sure one day I will, but for now the sentimental value of the gift means it remains unopened.

As has been proved since, Carlo's generosity never extends to when our sides face each other on the pitch.

They really punished us in Edinburgh, although I know there were other factors that contributed to our performance that day and it was a friendly. And then back in September they got the better of us in Italy in a superb football match.

I hate losing as much as anyone, but on that day I could not hate our performance. I thought we acquitted ourselves really well. It was the sort of performance that under most circumstances and against most teams would be good enough to win.

I have plenty of reference points when it comes to highlighting our opponent's quality tonight. The games we played last season were probably the toughest I can remember, in Naples and Liverpool.

The matches are so intense, physically and mentally. It's a battle for body and mind when we play them.

But I think it's important to realise they respect us also. The game we won here last season, by a single goal, I think we absolutely deserved to. The games we lost over there, we could easily have got more from.

So on the field it is a mutual respect for two clubs who really deserve to be considered among the best in Europe.

As well as Carlo, I welcome the Napoli players, staff, officials and supporters to Anfield. I hope, other than the 90-plus minutes on the pitch, they enjoy their visit to this very special city and region.

From our perspective we come into tonight after a really challenging game at the weekend.

Like Napoli, who drew against AC Milan, we faced a tough away trip after the international break. This is never easy. I read some of my quotes back after and it reminded me as always that the immediate reaction is never as complete as when you have had time to process.

When I factor in all the circumstances and all the challenges it really was a tremendous performance from this group of players. We were dominant, brave, smart, and we thoroughly deserved to win in my view.

The lack of preparation time for the game is a big reason why sometimes the tempo and rhythm isn't what we expect of ourselves, but the truth is we played well and we got our rewards. It never felt anything other than we were in control and I like this. It's important.

It will be important again this evening. The previous games against Napoli have shown us we must always have the highest of concentration – from minute one to minute 95, and beyond if needed. A game against a team of Napoli's quality is never done until the final whistle is blown. We have been very good this season in demonstrating our attributes in this area.

People make a big point about the late goals – and yes, they are cool – but what is also cool is showing control and managing a game in those dying moments. We have been outstanding at this so far.

The key attribute to achieve this is maximum concentration – we will need it again and again.

Finally, tonight can be a decisive game in the group depending on how the result goes. I think Anfield will recognise this and perform accordingly. I am a big believer that if you can achieve something at the earliest opportunity you should look to do so. So we must all give our best to get the job done tonight.

A talented, well-led, committed opponent awaits us. They have passionate and noisy backing from their supporters. Therefore we should not just look to match them – we must do better.

That's all of us: players, supporters and management. Give our all and we will have a night to remember, I hope.

Liverpool 1, SSC Napoli 1

Goal: Lovren (65)

Line-up (4-3-3): Alisson, Gomez (Oxlade-Chamberlain 57), Lovren, Van Dijk, Robertson, Henderson (c), Fabinho (Wijnaldum 19), Milner (Alexander-Arnold 78), Salah, Firmino, Mane. Subs not used: Adrian, Lallana, Shaqiri, Origi

Jürgen's post-match reaction: 'The situation in the table is still open. A lot of people around Liverpool think, 'Now we have to play again and have to put in everything we have.' But it was never different. It's not brilliant but it's okay. Let's use the situation.'

v Brighton
Saturday, November 30th, 3pm

'WE ARE REALLY 'IN IT' NOW. WE DON'T SEE THIS AS A BURDEN BUT AS AN OPPORTUNITY. SO LET'S GRASP IT'

Premier League

GOOD afternoon and welcome back to Anfield for our Premier League game against Brighton & Hove Albion.

I'm pleased we are back here today, given it is such a quick turnaround from Wednesday's intense game.

I love it when we play at Anfield and I never ever get tired of that feeling.

It's important we all park any thoughts of the Champions League for the time being. I felt going into the game midweek it would go to Matchday Six again and so it proved. So it's all cool, but that competition is further down the road now and therefore must not be in our thoughts or vision.

The focus must be 100 per cent on today and today only – a really tough game against a really well-coached team with excellent players.

I'm sure the Brighton staff and players enjoyed Wednesday night, because they will have seen the amount we had to put in to get any sort of result. But I'm sure they know our quality as well as our commitment and therefore will also know that they get a Liverpool with their best face today.

That is what we have to do: be at our very best.

My preference would always be that we perform to our maximum, but the truth is the last two matches have maybe not been that entirely. There are very understandable factors for this so I am fine with it.

Although this team never requires a nudge to make

sure we remember our responsibilities, it's not always a bad thing to have a reminder that we need to keep striving to produce our very best if we want to succeed in each contest.

The competitions we play in are so challenging. The Premier League is rightly considered the most competitive of any in the world and it's because of fixtures like today.

We face a team with players who are of the highest quality. They are organised and motivated to the highest level. Their determination and desire will be as high as you can imagine.

That's why the Premier League is the competition it is. You fight for everything – you give your all – or you get nothing.

I welcome Graham Potter, his players, staff, officials and supporters of Brighton to Anfield today.

Although relatively young in management terms, Graham has great experience already, having started his coaching career nearly a decade ago.

He was very highly rated in Sweden where he was admired for his innovative approach and progressive ideas.

When he came to the UK he did a really good job at Swansea City in some difficult circumstances, I would say, and has been superb since joining Brighton. It's a fantastic club with some top players and it's pleasing to see Graham take on the brilliant work done by Chris Hughton.

Obviously I hope the visit to Anfield is not nice for the 90-plus minutes for Graham and his team, but after that I wish them well for the rest of this campaign.

Returning to the main theme of this column, which is being at our best: it's important for all of us with a Liverpool heart today.

Make no mistake, this is a big test for all of us. Players, manager and coaches, but also supporters. It is on me and the players to make sure we set the agenda and the tone with how we approach it. We must be full of energy and positive aggression.

As a team we must be the embodiment of intensity in our approach. And if we do that I am 100 per cent certain our amazing supporters will be there with us – the wind at our back.

We can make Anfield as special and inspirational as any game since I have been here if we want to do this. We have to play our part, but I think if there was a game where energy from the Anfield crowd would be good, I'd identify this one.

We are really 'in it' now, in terms of the intense run of games. We don't see this as a burden but as an opportunity. So let's grasp it – make it special – and enjoy being back in our home together for a football match to remember.

Liverpool 2, Brighton 1

Goals: Van Dijk (18, 24)

Line-up (4-3-3): Alisson, Alexander-Arnold, Lovren, Van Dijk, Robertson, Oxlade-Chamberlain (Adrian 78), Henderson (c), Wijnaldum, Salah (Lallana 69), Firmino (Origi 76), Mane. Subs not used: Milner, Keita, Gomez, Shaqiri

Jürgen's post-match reaction: 'In a lot of moments [it went well], always knowing about the very specific quality of Brighton; they don't care too much about the opponent they play. We scored two nice goals after set-pieces, really wonderful goals, but the biggest chances we had were from open play. That was really, really good how we played there – we could have, should have finished it off in that period but we didn't and you have the most tricky result. If you think about a lead in the game, then 1-0 and everybody is clear, completely focused, everything is clear, 3-0, it is not decided but at least a little bolster, but 2-0 is like it is. Second half it was hard work again and the boys put in another incredible shift. Of course, life became more complicated with the red card and the change we had to make. We had to bring on a frozen goalkeeper pretty much! I am very, very happy about the effort the boys put in again, I'm really happy and proud about the desire the boys showed. The red card made it a really special win, to be honest.'

Post-match notes

Goalkeeper Alisson received Liverpool's first red card of the season in the Premier League.

DEC

2019

Lots of games, lots of travelling but Jürgen and his troops were able to add a very special trophy to their silverware haul and tighten their grip on top spot in the Premier League

4th: Everton (PL) H
7th: Bournemouth (PL) A
10th: RB Salzburg (CL) A
14th: Watford (PL) H
17th: Aston Villa (CC) A
18th: CF Monterrey (CWC) N
21st: Flamengo (CWC) N
26th: Leicester City (PL) A
29th: Wolverhampton W (PL) H

v Everton
Wednesday, December 4th, 8.15pm

‘I LOVE THE PASSION AROUND THIS GAME. I LOVE HOW MUCH IT MATTERS TO BOTH OF US’

Premier League

December 2019

GOOD evening and welcome back to Anfield for our Premier League fixture against our neighbours Everton.

Due to print deadlines I am writing these notes ahead of our opponent's game being played on Sunday at Leicester City, so I'm unable to add any context of the effect of that result on this evening.

However, I actually don't think it matters a great deal, because of the nature of this fixture. It's a Merseyside derby and therefore every minute of every other fixture this season is almost irrelevant.

When the whistle goes tonight it's two fierce rivals, who share a city, going head-to-head to do the very best for their supporters. My experience of this fixture and derby games in general teaches me our current standings in the league will count for nothing.

It is no exaggeration to say these games are the most competitive we face each season. Be it league or cup matches, the feeling around them is different and it is special. You only have to look at last season and how close the games were.

Yes, it is factual to point out that the number of points available for both teams is the same as when we play Brighton or Bournemouth – the fixtures either side of tonight for us – but the simple mathematics doesn't do justice to the occasion.

I love the passion around this game. I love how much it matters to both of us. I love that it's an obsession for both sets of supporters and therefore we, as a team, who have the responsibility to perform, must be respectful of that.

It can never be written off as 'just another game'. Again, from my experiences, Everton buy into the emotion of it really well – and so far in my time here, I feel we have as well.

These contests are about aggression and intensity. But by aggression I mean the positive aspect of it, not the negative. It's about being aggressive in your intent to be positive and brave. Show courage in decision-making. Be aggressive in the amount of yourself you will give to get the result.

I hate the idea it's about physical aggression aimed at an opponent – that is absolutely not okay and does not belong in this game.

There are so many positive ways to demonstrate intensity during the 90-plus minutes. Run harder than you normally would, be more concentrated, sacrifice more for the team, channel your emotions for the good of the group and not as an individual.

You enjoy occasions like these, in a team context, when you make them about what the collective can achieve together. It is a pertinent point to make at the moment because of the importance of our squad and each player in it for what we look to do here at Liverpool.

There has been focus recently on Fabinho being unavailable for a period. Obviously now Alisson is also not involved tonight, but for different reasons. I have never wavered from my belief that you can only be successful in the modern game if you have a squad of players all of whom recognise their importance and value.

We are in the period now where every minute on the pitch of each player is just so valuable to us. If any member of our squad lessens their contribution by even the smallest of percentages, for the shortest amount of time, we will achieve nothing.

I see the influence that all of our players have on what we do on a day-to-day basis. I get that those outside of Melwood don't have the same opportunity that my coaches and I have. But in the coming days, weeks and months that will of course change. And I have total belief the contribution of the entire squad will only enhance us, because of what I see on the training pitch.

There are so many players in our ranks who, until now, I have no reasonable explanation to give for why they haven't started more matches. So many have deserved to and my admiration for them as people and professionals could not be higher.

Turning back to today's opponents, I welcome Marco Silva, his players, staff, officials and supporters of Everton for the short trip to Anfield.

Marco is such a fierce competitor and I know he will relish the opportunity to bring his team here and get a result their supporters want. The games I have faced against sides managed by Marco have always been so difficult. Against his teams you need to be on it for the entire 90-plus minutes or you will struggle.

We expect Everton to come with purpose and belief and we must be ready. Nobody reading this needs me to tell them that the away end at Anfield will be full of noise and passion. So, it's a proper game and one that unless you give everything you have, you will be exposed. We will not allow that to happen from our perspective. We respect the opponent and the fixture. It's big and it matters.

Finally, to something more serious than any football game, even one as anticipated as the Merseyside derby. It feels appropriate that this game takes place tonight given that the courage and fortitude of the Hillsborough victims, families and survivors is again at the forefront of our thoughts.

Even though a football rivalry divides our two clubs, support for the cause of those affected by Hillsborough is a unifying factor at all times. When I learned about the tragedy before coming to this club, a recurring theme was the support Everton and Evertonians gave at the time and have always given since. This was evident again last week.

There are people far more qualified and more important than me to speak on what happened in the past weeks and if people want informed opinion they should read it from the people who have followed and advocated on behalf of the victims, families and survivors for decades. But, from this current team, I want to send my love to the families in particular and let them know they are always in our thoughts.

It is with this in mind we should look to create a positive, joyful atmosphere inside our home tonight.

Enjoying the rivalry can be about showing how much we want it for our club and how much we appreciate our own players. The energy inside Anfield should always be a positive one and tonight gives a great chance to demonstrate that again.

We all know how much we want the right result this evening, but we also know to achieve it we must work – players, supporters and management. We must create the situation where the performance and outcome is the one we want. We know our jobs, so now is the time to do them.

Liverpool 5, Everton 2

Goals: Origi (6, 31), Shaqiri (17), Mane (45), Wijnaldum (90)

Line-up (4-3-3): Adrian, Alexander-Arnold (Gomez 83), Lovren, Van Dijk, Robertson, Lallana (Henderson 72), Wijnaldum, Milner (c), Shaqiri, Origi (Firmino 73), Mane. Subs not used: Kelleher, Keita, Oxlade-Chamberlain, Salah

Jürgen's post-match reaction: 'Good – really, really good, especially in the circumstances I created pretty much by myself with the line-up. Making five changes can lead to some problems, of course. I didn't see any of them. We have to make changes, that's clear; probably some people were not too happy that we did that before a derby but we cannot make differences on that. It was clear it would be a really intense game so we needed fresh legs, as many as we could get. The only two boys I didn't bring tonight were Joe [Gomez] and Naby [Keita] and both – with Joe you saw it and Naby I can tell you – are in outstanding shape. It was only me not being brave enough to make [those changes] as well. But what the boys made of this difficult game was exceptional. We scored incredible goals. We had to fight. A few things didn't work out defensively. First, we probably surprised them with our system; then, they didn't surprise us but we couldn't adapt as quickly as possible as necessary to their little system change. We wanted to wait until half-time – I was fine with 4-1, I was not fine with 4-2. But then we adapted to the system. It was an intense game but we controlled it much more again, scored a sensational fifth goal and job done – all good.'

Post-match notes

This win saw Liverpool set a new club record of 32 consecutive league matches without defeat.

The win also saw Klopp reach 100 league wins faster than any manager in Liverpool history.

Saturday, December 7th, 3pm
Premier League
Bournemouth 0, Liverpool 3

Goals: Oxlade-Chamberlain (35), Keita (44), Salah (54)

Line-up (4-3-3): Alisson, Gomez, Van Dijk, Robertson (Jones 76), Lovren (Alexander-Arnold 40), Milner, Keita, Henderson (c), Oxlade-Chamberlain (Shaqiri 87), Firmino, Salah. Subs not used: Adrian, Elliott, Mane, Origi

Jürgen's post-match reaction: 'I feel for Eddie because you can lose against us obviously, that can happen, but then losing [Nathan] Ake and [Callum] Wilson [to injury] on a day like this [is difficult]. We scored wonderful goals, had more chances, did really well. We were really uncomfortable to play and from the 3-0 on, we controlled the game absolutely. Nothing really happened any more. I didn't want to see any unnecessary risks because when you lose the ball it's not a problem in football but it's not a time for players to chase constantly. Maybe it was not the most exciting but it was necessary. Yeah, it was an absolutely super performance, super individual performances and the team performance was just really mature and professional.'

Post-match notes

Despite Liverpool's strong start to the season, this was their first clean sheet in 15 games.

Tuesday, December 10th, 5.55pm
UEFA Champions League,
RB Salzburg 0, Liverpool 2

Goals: Keita (57), Salah (58)

Line-up (4-3-3): Alisson, Alexander-Arnold, Lovren (Gomez 53), Van Dijk, Robertson, Keita (Origi 87), Henderson (c), Wijnaldum, Mane, Firmino (Milner 75), Salah. Subs not used: Adrian, Jones, Shaqiri, Oxlade-Chamberlain

Jürgen's post-match reaction: 'I know how people see it – you think being the best team in Austria is 'okay'. Then you see how good they are, how good they were in the first game, and then you could come here as the current Champions League winner and misunderstand that situation. I really love it that my team is so smart that they listen and they put in a shift like that. Salzburg was unbelievably strong, especially in the first half, but we were ready for that fight. We could have scored in the first half already, maybe should have scored. In the second half it's not easy to keep that intensity; we scored the goals, could have scored more but really massive respect for Jesse [Marsch] and Salzburg for what they did here. [On Salah's incredible tight-angled finish] Such a decisive and very difficult finish, that probably says much more about him than all of the other goals he has scored. So, staying concentrated, belief in the next moment, it was brilliant. A very, very difficult goal but a sensational finish.'

v Watford
Saturday, December 14th, 12.30pm

'IF AT ANY POINT WE ARE KNOCKED TO THE CANVAS I KNOW WE WILL GET BACK ON OUR FEET'

Premier League

GOOD afternoon and welcome back to Anfield for our Premier League game against Watford.

As part of today's matchday we are celebrating all the great work the team does at the LFC Foundation – the club's official charity. This will be the fifth LFC Foundation Day and this year they are showcasing their programmes that help to support over 28,000 people across the city.

To find out more about the Foundation's great work then give them a follow on Twitter @LFCFoundation.

Today is our most important game of the season – it is that simple. We are in the good position we are at the moment because our focus is always that the only game that matters is the next one.

In the build-up to today there have been questions about the other competitions we are about to be involved in, but I can tell you hand-on-heart that the only thing we have looked at ahead of today is Watford. They are such a strong opponent that if we lose even one per cent attention on the threat they pose we will not get the result we want.

The Premier League is so strong and so competitive, every contest is a cup final. My understanding is that describing it as such in this country is a cliché but I'm sorry, it is true.

It is what makes this competition unique in the world and when you factor in how relentlessly the matches come at you it's one of the biggest tests also, I think. There is no respite for us, in the sporting sense, and this is absolutely fine. We don't ask for a second that anyone feels sorry for us. If anyone did it would be silly.

We are involved in amazing things, an occupation we are so privileged to do. We get incredible opportunities and rewards. We do something that brings joy to others – this is very cool.

So we are totally aware of how blessed we are, but at the same time in this moment it is work. This is a job to do. We love our work – we are fortunate to do it – but we have a responsibility to treat it with respect.

There will be many who talk about this fixture today with a lack of respect, I am sure. We are 1,000 per cent not part of this conversation. The funny thing is, anyone showing disregard for how tough this will be, are disrespecting both teams, not just one of us.

I am not silly, so I am aware people will point to our respective positions in the Premier League and make assumptions. But we do not and never will.

I welcome Nigel Pearson, his players, staff, officials and supporters of Watford back to Anfield.

For Nigel, in particular, it is great to see him back managing in England and the Premier League specifically. A very smart appointment. Brilliant manager, knows the league, knows this situation also.

I remember the job Nigel did at Leicester City, when

everyone in the country had written them off as being certainties for relegation. He stayed calm, he kept his players together, he channelled all the right emotions, and he did a quite incredible job in keeping them up. Honestly, the respect his fellow managers had for the job he did then could not be higher.

And his Leicester team achieved that target by winning games and taking points from stadiums and opponents where people were quick to write them off and dismiss their chances.

The other factor in Nigel's favour is that he is taking over a squad packed with quality players. Their achievements last season, in reaching the FA Cup final and also what they did in the Premier League, showed their quality.

They are nearly all still together, so this is a very good set of players, with an experienced leader and they have the highest motivation in this moment. So it's a big game and a big job to do.

But, as I always say, the really cool thing is we are a very good team ourselves and our attitude is such we won't allow any distraction in our focus.

My players live in the moment, they are totally in our situation. It comes back to what I was saying earlier about this being 'work'. I love that my players embrace their responsibility as professionals. I see it day in and day out. The respect they show their work is so high.

The standards they set of themselves could not be greater. They are their harshest judge and jury.

This is a group of players who have tunnel vision and it's always centred on the next challenge. They play each match with the attitude of it being the only thing that matters in that moment.

Of course, we all know at some point this season we will have a setback. We don't think it will be nine months of sunlight and warmth. Clouds will come and in those moments we will need to be ready to react.

We have seen it already in games this season. We do not sail always on calm waters, despite our results. We have taken some big punches and kept moving forward. If at any point we are knocked to the canvas, I know we will get back on our feet well before the 10 count is done – and I also know we will be ready to come out swinging. This is us. This is what we do.

This season, like all at this level, is a fight. It is not a party. It is intense. It is constant. It is a challenge. It is work. It is work we love and work that fulfils us.

It is absolutely okay for the supporters to embrace the joy and it is fantastic to see how much they love what we do. But they also are well-educated and they know we are not in a scenario where we can afford to stop and feel any sense of accomplishment. If we fell into that trap – as a team, supporters or club – we achieve nothing.

So for the supporters I say: let's keep going. Together – this collective force. We focus all we have on today and facing a really tough opponent whom we respect. All of us – every single person in Anfield with a Liverpool heart beating in their chests – has to turn up today with the attitude of giving all we have for this 90-plus minutes. Leave nothing in the locker, make it our best day. I know we can do this.

Very finally, as we are not back at Anfield until after the 25th of December, I would like to wish everyone a very happy and peaceful Christmas period. These are difficult times across the world and it is so sad that so many look for what divides us, rather than a sense of community and society that can bring us together.

We have a supporter-base with such rich diversity that many will observe this time of year in their own way, and some will choose not to at all. It's why, for me, football is so great in the team and dressing-room sense.

In a dressing room you don't look at someone and see colour, creed, sexuality or anything of that nature. You see a friend, a team-mate, someone who you can help and someone who can help you. Someone that by working together you can have better collective experiences than if you tried to do it on your own.

Therefore, however you observe this time of year, I think we should take the best values of football and the best values of LFC and make sure we remember we don't live on this planet alone and our existence is made so much better by not walking alone and instead showing love and compassion to those around us.

Enjoy the game.

Liverpool 2, Watford 0

Goals: Salah (38, 90)

Line-up (4-2-3-1): Alisson, Alexander-Arnold, Gomez, Van Dijk, Milner, Henderson (c), Wijnaldum (Robertson 59), Shaqiri (Oxlade-Chamberlain 70), Firmino (Origi 88), Mane, Salah. Subs not used: Adrian, Keita, Lallana, Williams

Jürgen's post-match reaction: 'At 1-0, you can never rely on the game being decided. No problem with that. In December and January especially, you need to show resilience – that's the most important thing. And we showed that, but Watford showed it as well. We had chances, we scored goals, but they had chances as well which they didn't score from – and that's for sure one reason why they are in the situation they are in. Two or three balls they missed. This time maybe now I can speak about, but the wind helped us today from time to time – I am pretty sure Sarr would have at least had a finish in the situation when he didn't hit the ball without the wind. It made the game tricky for both sides, that's clear, but it helps them a little bit more than us usually in those situations. Ali was for 85 minutes really doing warm-up exercises, but in these [other] five minutes he was really important and just showed what a goalie he is; he is unbelievable. We had to fight, that's what we did and that's why we won. All good.'

Tuesday, December 17th, 7.45pm
Carabao Cup quarter-final
Aston Villa 5, Liverpool 0

Line-up (4-3-3): Kelleher, Hoever (Norris 82), Van den Berg, Boyes, Gallacher, Kane, Chirivella (c), Christie-Davies (Clarkson 77), Elliott, Longstaff (Bearne 65), Hill. Subs not used: Winterbottom, Clayton, Dixon-Bonner, Stewart

Jürgen's post-match reaction [speaking in Qatar]: 'Our kids were offensively outstanding. I saw a lot of stuff they did that was brilliant. You wear a Liverpool shirt so you have to play a certain way. That's what the kids did.'

Neil Critchley's post-match reaction: 'We had some information at half-time from the manager – basically to keep playing the way we were playing, keep being brave, keep doing what we were doing. So he was out there watching with the staff and the players and I hope, and I'm sure he will be, he is proud of the way we played tonight. We played like a Liverpool team and I think the supporters really appreciated the players' efforts'

Post-match notes

With the first-team squad in Qatar for the FIFA Club World Cup, Neil Critchley was manager for this Carabao Cup tie. The starting line-up was the youngest in Liverpool history (an average of 19 years and 183 days).

Wednesday, December 18th, 5.30pm
FIFA Club World Cup semi-final
Monterrey 1, Liverpool 2
Khalifa International Stadium

Goals: Keita (12), Firmino (90+1)

Line-up (4-3-3): Alisson, Milner (Alexander-Arnold 74), Gomez, Henderson (c), Robertson, Lallana, Keita, Oxlade-Chamberlain, Shaqiri (Mane 68), Salah, Origi (Firmino 85). Subs not used: Adrian, Lonergan, Jones, Williams

Klopp was delighted to win a place in the FIFA Club World Cup final following Roberto Firmino's late winner in Doha.

On his side's hard-fought win...

I don't think it was possible to be a different way. The hard way we saw now with a couple of games here in this tournament and obviously each team is here to represent the country, the continent, whatever, and try everything to be successful. The opponent tonight did exactly the same, they fought really hard. We had problems before the game, we knew that we will have some problems in the game as well, it was clear. But I really think the boys did exceptionally well because we had so many strange things. It was the most offensive midfield I've probably ever lined up in a competitive game, then Hendo and Joe Gomez together as a centre-half pairing – Hendo's first time at centre-half, what a game! We controlled the game for a long period and then they came with the set-piece. With the set-piece, where it was clear that we were not too tall today, I think Funes Mori scored the goal and usually a player in that situation is offside when you play against us. In this case, he was not offside – that's one thing. Then counter-attacks, long balls, stuff like this, that's what they had and then we had Ali in these moments, which helps obviously a lot, or we defended in a different way. I am really overly-happy with the performance because I knew before the game that it will be really tough and the boys did really well.

On the spirit and determination of his team...
I was actually afraid of the extra-time, to be honest! So I was more than happy when Bobby scored that goal. We had to do a few changes because we had no other options, but we wanted some other changes for the line-up. It means we left Trent out, Bobby out and Sadio out, so that gives us then the opportunity when the game is not decided to make a decision. That Bobby scored the goal is just wonderful. I saw the goal but not that the ball went in because so many players were in between, I just saw the reaction of the opposite goalkeeper and he was not too happy, so I started celebrating. It was really, really cool.

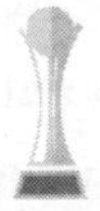

Saturday, December 21st, 5.30pm
FIFA Club World Cup final
Liverpool 1 Flamengo 0
Khalifa International Stadium

Goal: Firmino (99)

Line-up (4-3-3): Alisson, Alexander-Arnold, Gomez, Van Dijk, Robertson, Henderson (c), Keita (Milner 100), Oxlade-Chamberlain (Lallana 75), Mane, Salah (Shaqiri 120+1), Firmino (Origi 105). Subs not used: Adrian, Lonergan, Wijnaldum, Jones, Hoever, Elliott, Van den Berg, Williams

Liverpool became world champions for the first time in the club's history. Klopp could be incredibly proud of his team's achievement.

On how it feels to be world champions...
It's great, really great. We are all exhausted from a really intense game. We had a few moments in the past when I really struggle to find the right words in not my native language for describing my respect for the boys, how they do it. It's incredible, it was an incredible performance in an incredibly difficult game against a good opponent. But we did so many good things it's unbelievable, so many good football moments. Everybody was for different reasons on the edge pretty much but I saw so

many sensationally good performances and I'm really happy, of course, for our supporters.

The atmosphere in the stadium was great, Flamengo supporters had the whole week a party week here and unfortunately maybe they cannot celebrate that much, but they should be proud of what they did and what their team did. But I think we deserved to win tonight, we were the better side. In some moments we had a really good goalie and in all the other moments we were the dominant team. I'm really happy.

On what winning the Club World Cup means for this team...

A wonderful night for us, the club, for everybody who is with us. There are always things, of course, that are not so positive because it was not the last game of the season and Oxlade-Chamberlain got injured in one situation. We play in five days again, so that's a tough period. But the boys – game after game after game – they really show their desire to make the next step, show their desire to win the next game, show their desire to win the next challenge and I'm really happy about that. Where will it lead us? I have no idea. For tonight, we couldn't do more than winning this game, winning it the first time for this wonderful club, the Club World Cup.

I said before the game I don't know exactly how it would feel. Now I can say it's outstanding, absolutely sensational. I'm so proud of the boys and it couldn't be better.

On his thoughts about the game...

I think in possession we did a lot stuff Flamengo didn't like. We played from like a defensive 4-4-2 system, they changed slightly and did Everton in the centre more and for that another player played the wing. But with the step-ins of our centre-halves, it made life difficult for them to defend these things. Joe Gomez, Virgil van Dijk stepped in midfield, could pass the ball on the wing and that's then difficult. You have to defend at your best to defend these situations. But how I said, it was a very intense game. For different reasons it was not our best game we ever played, but it was more than good enough to deserve the win tonight for 120 minutes unfortunately – but even that is absolutely okay.

We spoke a lot about what it means for European teams to win this competition and now we are here. If you really want to win it we have to show that to everybody and I think my players showed that from the first second, that's the most important thing.

From a tactical point of view, I have to watch the game again, but I just think we were the better team. Physically, both teams suffered tonight and maybe the extra-time was slightly fresher or whatever. The goalie of Flamengo had cramp and that shows they had a lot of games. I couldn't respect them more. The season they played is exceptional, absolutely exceptional. But tonight it was not that, tonight it was about better decision-making in decisive moments and try to win the game. We did that and I'm really happy with that.

On the week in Qatar...

If we wouldn't have played the semi-final here then we would have played against Aston Villa one day earlier. If we wouldn't have played tonight here, we would have played at West Ham, so same number of games and situation. The difference here is the climate, even if when it was not as warm as probably Europeans would have expected in the moment, is still something we have to adapt to. You could see that in each session it's just different.

We are used to different weather conditions and that was difficult for other teams and for us as well. But that's the only thing that is special. Apart from that, we had the same number of games like we would have had at home. We will play the West Ham game – we don't know it yet – but in any point in the New Year and that will be then tough to find a moment for when we can play that game. But until then we will not think about that. We have the same number of games like Leicester had and Man City had and other teams had, so all good. We have to make sure that we come home safely and then recover on the plane if possible and then prepare for the Leicester game.

On Roberto Firmino's contribution to the team...

The best thing about our three boys up there and all the others, if one is not scoring then the other one is scoring or the other two are scoring.

Divock Origi, for example, and nobody is talking about him, scored incredibly important goals. Xherdan Shaqiri has scored incredibly important goals last year or set them up. Mo Salah scores for us an incredible number of goals, all of them very important, but not always. Then Sadio is stepping up and scores incredibly important goals.

Now here, we needed obviously Bobby's goal and here they are. I couldn't be more happy for him that he could score that goal because before the game we spoke a lot about what this competition means to Brazil, to South American people and especially Brazilian people. And we have two Brazilians and he's one of them. It means the world to him and it helped us a lot. On top of that, it was a sensational goal, completely calm. You see the last goal helped to bring these things back and I'm really, really delighted for him.

Thursday, December 26th, 8pm
Premier League
Leicester City 0, Liverpool 4

Goals: Firmino (31,74), Milner (71pen), Alexander-Arnold (78)

Line-up (4-3-3): Alisson, Alexander-Arnold, Gomez, Van Dijk, Robertson, Wijnaldum, Henderson (c) (Lallana 82), Keita (Milner 70), Mane, Salah (Origi 70), Firmino. Subs not used: Adrian, Williams, Shaqiri, Jones

Jürgen's post-match reaction: 'How good they are, everybody knows, how dangerous they can be, everybody knows, and my boys just played a very good football game. Really, really completely focused, in most moments really well organised. Blocked shots – I don't know how many shots they had on target tonight, probably not too many. And then playing football ourselves, so the first goal was obviously brilliant but the bigger chances we had before that but didn't score. After, the 2-0 penalty, it was a corner, Divock Origi came a second before on the pitch and I think if he's not there then the defender probably sees the ball a bit better and can react differently. Millie came on a second before and could finish the situation, that helped. Third goal, worldie, just completely cool and composed: a super ball from Trent and Bobby with the super finish. And then Trent with the fourth with a super finish. It was a really good football game, but we had to be good otherwise we would have lost here.'

v Wolverhampton Wanderers
Sunday, December 29th, 4.30pm

'IT'S TOUGH AT A CLUB LIKE LIVERPOOL TO ACHIEVE SOMETHING FOR THE FIRST TIME'

Premier League

GOOD evening and welcome back to Anfield for our Premier League match against Wolverhampton Wanderers.

Because of the Christmas period this column is being written before I've even had a chance to think about the team selection for Leicester City on Boxing Day, let alone reflect on the result. Likewise with our opponent, who I know faced a really tough game at home.

Whatever the outcome in those matches, it won't change the fact today is an incredibly challenging game and one to relish and look forward to.

It's impossible as I write this to analyse the impact of our trip to Qatar for the FIFA Club World Cup. Of course, winning it was fantastic and a real honour. As a lot of the players said before we went, it's tough at a club like Liverpool to achieve something for the first time, because of our successful history. But that's what we did and I couldn't be prouder of the players for their attitude and approach.

We enjoyed ourselves in the dressing room after the game, as you may have seen from the pictures and videos the boys took.

But what struck me most was how quickly the boys drew a line and immediately switched focus to being ready for the contests to come. I shouldn't keep being surprised by this group, in the positive sense of surprise, but somehow they keep doing it.

I can't think of any more competitive and intense contests than Leicester, Wolves and Sheffield United over this period.

All three teams are built on energy and positive aggression. But – so are we. So this is cool.

This may have already been written in the aftermath of Leicester for all I know, but I'm sure there will be plenty of people externally ready to comment on what effect the Doha trip will have on the Premier League campaign.

I can answer this, regardless of the results: none! Because we won't allow it. This group of players know they set their own agenda and their own benchmarks.

They know they have the capacity to decide if going into a game we allow ourselves to feel fatigue or we choose to be fresh in body and mind. It's a choice we can make – we have the power to decide our own approach.

I'm not stupid and we know what faces us in this particular period is a big, big test. But this is the Premier League and our ambition is to be the most successful team in it and that means rising to meet every challenge.

Talking about a particular subject is completely different to using it as an excuse. And these players have a 'no excuse culture' running through them.

We will have setbacks, we will lose games, of course we will. This isn't because of failings we may have but because the quality of opponent is so high. But we will never look to external factors to explain it, no matter how legitimate they may appear.

Our approach must always be about opportunity. To win the FIFA Club World Cup for the first time in our history was an opportunity and we took it. To come back to the fierce intensity of competition in the Premier League on the back of that – to this schedule – is an opportunity for us to perform if we choose to approach it as such, and we will.

That is what I have seen from the players since we came back together in July and August. We set our agenda. We decide what is possible. It is in our gift to view the 'pressure' we are supposedly all under as a positive, not a negative.

Jordan Henderson spoke about this a lot last season and he was right. Replace the notion of pressure with opportunity. The right sort of pressure, which is linked to achieving something special, is a motivator and not a backpack to carry. Seeing pressure as opportunity can lift you up, rather than weigh you down. So this is where we are at as a team during this period. And it applies whether we win, lose or draw in certain games.

This evening we face an unbelievably strong opponent and I really think it has the potential to be an amazing football match for those who love this special game of ours.

I welcome Nuno Espírito Santo to Anfield, along with

his players, staff, officials and supporters of Wolves.

What a job Nuno is doing! My respect and admiration could not be higher. The way they play, the success they achieve.

For what he's achieved in the little under three years he's been here, Nuno must be considered one of the most successful managers in England in this moment for what he has done and how he has done it.

They are an incredible team with great players – the perfect approach. They have the respect of everyone in the Premier League and when you face them you know that if you are even a tiny percentage below your best you will get punished. That's the mark of a top side.

I know my players respect Wolves, but it's a healthy respect and one built on recognising our own qualities also and putting them first in our thoughts. This is why tonight is such an exciting game and one that, if I wasn't working for either club, I would want to watch as someone who loves great football.

We will give it all we have and look to show our best face. We want to come back to Anfield and put on a display our supporters can find joy in.

This period is a challenge for players and fans alike. I thank our amazing fans for everything they sacrifice to follow us, be it Aston Villa for the Carabao Cup, Doha or Leicester for a late kick-off on Boxing Day. It is our job to match their commitment.

I'm sure Anfield will be on its toes tonight and when it is, there is no better place for a game such as this.

Liverpool 1, Wolves 0

Goal: Mane (42)

Line-up (4-2-3-1): Alisson, Alexander-Arnold, Gomez, Van Dijk, Robertson, Henderson (c), Wijnaldum (Milner 86), Lallana (Keita 67), Mane, Salah, Firmino (Origi 86). Subs not used: Adrian, Jones, Elliott, Williams

Jürgen's post-match reaction: 'It was [a hard-fought game], it was indeed. No surprise, Wolves are a proper, proper team with a lot of strength, but in the first half we controlled the game like we wanted, like we should. We had chances, scored the goal. We had to defend, the counter-attacking threat is massive but we defended it well. Then we scored the goal. I think Nuno was not happy with the VAR procedure probably, I am not sure if it was with the decision. If it would be easy to win that number of games a lot more teams would have done it. It is not easy and you have to fight with all you have. Sometimes we have more and sometimes less and the boys do that all the time, so I couldn't be more proud of what they did again. To get that result over the line is just impressive and I am really happy about it.'

Post-match notes

The Reds finished the year with 98 points from a possible 111 and made it 50 Premier League home games unbeaten.

JAN

2020

A strong end to 2019 was followed by an equally powerful start to the new year. Any worries Klopp had about the heavy schedule of taxing matches and tiring travelling would be forgotten as five Premier League wins out of five strengthened his side's grip on top spot

2nd: Sheffield United (PL) H
5th: Everton (FA) H
11th: Tottenham (PL) A
19th: Manchester United (PL) H
23rd: Wolverhampton W (PL) A
26th: Shrewsbury Town (FA) A
29th: West Ham (PL) A

v Sheffield United
Thursday, January 2nd, 8pm

'I'M NOT IN THE REVIEWING MOOD. WE'RE RIGHT IN THE MIDDLE OF SOMETHING, NOWHERE NEAR AN ENDING'

Premier League

GOOD evening and welcome back to Anfield for our Premier League fixture against Sheffield United.

I would like to start this column by wishing everyone a Happy New Year. I spent a lot of the post-match interviews after Wolves being asked about my reflections on 2019 and even though it was a year with a lot of happy memories, from a football perspective there isn't anything 'new' we have to think about. There is no pause and certainly no stop.

Our professional life works in 'seasons' rather than calendar years, so in this moment I am not in the reviewing mood. We are exactly halfway through a league campaign, with two cup competitions to fight for also. So, we are right in the middle of something and nowhere near an ending.

The only reviewing we are doing in this moment is with regards to our next opponent. We have reviewed Sheffield United extensively, but that is all.

I spoke after the Wolves game about how the team and the supporters are a unit in this moment in how they view the current situation and I think this is an important point.

The world we live in means that we are constantly presented with invitations to see conclusions where there are none. For the players, my staff and I, it is very easy to maintain the concentration we need because of how hard the challenges we face are.

How do you stay focused? That's easy – look at how strong Sheffield United are. If you were in danger of distraction, spending time analysing our opponents soon sharpens the senses.

I referenced the supporters after Sunday's game because I think their understanding and intelligence was a critical factor in us getting the result we did. We have all long since learned we can achieve nothing alone, but the Wolves game was a perfect case study in terms of the importance of players and supporters being one.

Anfield is our greatest asset because of the role our supporters play. They are in this moment with us and they know their job so well.

Like the players, it's important we maintain this now. Arrive at every game with the attitude of making the 90-plus minutes the most important of their lives. Don't look ahead, don't dwell on what is behind. The here and now is our everything on the pitch and in the stands.

I know we need it again tonight. This game is going to be a battle where every second matters.

I welcome Chris Wilder, his players, staff, officials and supporters of Sheffield United to Anfield.

There is nothing I could write here that would appropriately reflect what Chris and his team have achieved over the past few seasons. It is an amazing story and one with more chapters to come clearly.

They strike me as a group who care not one bit what anyone outside of their circle think of them. I love this.

The things I hear and read about them say to me that they don't get the credit their quality deserves. I read a lot about outstanding character. I read a lot about their determination and fight. But this does them such a disservice. They are smart in every department and that clearly comes from the manager.

The game we played against them in Sheffield was probably our toughest of the season. And it wasn't because we made it hard for ourselves – we were very good in that game. But Sheffield United were outstanding, individually and collectively. If anything, they have improved even more since then, so they arrive here at Anfield a more dangerous opponent.

They will have a plan for us and we must be ready. We have to out-fight and out-think them. If we don't, we won't get the result we all want. Against teams as good as this, that is what happens.

I know my team will approach this contest with the perfect attitude, so that is a big reason for us to have confidence and be positive.

These players are loving the intensity of the moment we are in. They are feeding off it and finding energy from it. We are in a moment now where we are tested to the maximum and everyone recognises the importance of their contribution.

I love how everyone sees their value. I made reference recently to only having three adult outfield players on the bench for the last game. This was not meant to be demeaning to the young boys at all, quite the opposite actually.

The contribution Curtis, Neco and Harvey make to this group is huge. And Ki-Jana, Sepp and Caoimhin – I could go on. Nat Phillips is back now and he also makes us stronger as a unit.

The level they bring to our training is why we can perform as we do in the matches. But it's more than just training. The three young boys on the bench at the weekend are all 'ready' if and when we need them – and we certainly will. This makes all the difference in the world when competing in the intense environment we do.

We are so blessed to have these brilliant young professionals at our club.

Tonight has the potential to be a wonderful occasion at Anfield, under the lights against an opponent who will bring their own energy. We all know there is another job to do. We all need to be at our best. We all know our importance and we know we can reflect that in how we are and how we conduct ourselves when the whistle goes and the ball starts to roll.

If we are all in the moment and give our best I believe we can have an evening we can all find joy in.

Liverpool 2, Sheffield United 0

Goals: Salah (4), Mane (64)

Line-up (4-3-3): Alisson, Alexander-Arnold, Gomez, Van Dijk, Robertson (Lallana 88), Milner, Henderson (c), Wijnaldum, Salah (Elliott 90+2), Firmino, Mane (Origi 78). Subs not used: Adrian, Phillips, Jones, Williams

Jürgen's post-match reaction: 'What I saw was a really good football game. I saw a game which we played in exactly the way you have to play against Sheffield United. The biggest and best thing the boys did tonight was that they didn't let our opponents get anything of the game, which is really difficult with the way they defend. But we did really well. Our passing was really good, we broke lines, our positioning was exceptional. The discipline in these things offensively was exceptional. Because of the way they set up, it's difficult to counter-press because they pass pretty much the first ball immediately into one of the two strikers. But still it was really good how we reacted – the centre-halves were spot on, Hendo around that was outstanding. These other moments they had and we didn't let them happen until pretty much after 75, 80 minutes when we started passing sloppily. Then you saw they were not broken after 80 minutes without possession. We could get concentrated again and controlled the game until the end.'

Post-match notes

This win ensured the Reds completed a calendar year unbeaten in the Premier League.

v Everton
Sunday, January 5th, 4.01pm

'IT FEELS LIKE WE'RE BANGING OUR HEADS AGAINST A BRICK WALL'

FA Cup third round

GOOD afternoon and welcome back to Anfield for our FA Cup tie against Everton.

Due to the schedule and print deadlines I am writing this column prior to our Premier League fixture against Sheffield United, therefore I'm unable to offer any context to that performance or result on today.

What I do know is for ourselves – and our opponent this afternoon – this game comes after an intense period which has tested all teams to the absolute limit.

Sometimes it feels like all I do is speak about the schedule and the ramifications of it. I think the English phrase is 'sounding like a broken record'. There is another English phrase also, regarding 'banging your head against a brick wall'.

It's been notable just how many managers and players have spoken out during the past fortnight and we can only hope that somewhere this feedback is being appropriately considered.

Just to be clear, no-one involved in football at our level feels sorry for ourselves or is looking for sympathy for our situation. We are immensely privileged to do what we do and get incredible rewards for it. We know we are blessed. And despite perceptions, the vast majority of us involved in the game come from very normal backgrounds, where we know the strains of real life far outweigh being asked to play a couple of football matches in quick succession.

Be it nurses or carers, emergency services, people who work in the service industry – we know there are millions and millions of people in this country who do jobs more worthy and beneficial than ours and are paid a fraction.

I have yet to meet anyone working in football who doesn't acknowledge this.

That said, I do think we are in a situation now that requires those in leadership positions in the game to come together and start looking for solutions to the schedule issue.

Again, so my views aren't misrepresented, no-one is saying we can't play the games. The question should be: is it right to and what is the impact on health and quality? For me the consequences are clear. It is the players and fans who ultimately suffer and football without these two groups is nothing.

If you follow a club and you make sacrifices, both in terms of personal finances and the even more precious commodity of time, then it is only right that you see a team give their very best. The present circumstances make that very difficult to do constantly. We still try, of course.

We pile more and more expectations onto the players.

We want them to be faster, stronger, braver, smarter. We want to see them at full-throttle. And, of course, this should be the case – it's what the supporters deserve.

But it is not possible to do this constantly without reasonable rest and recovery time. Players are human beings – we would all do well to remember this, I think.

The retort to people like me and my fellow managers when we say these things is "Well, what is your solution?" It's a fair comment but it's being aimed at the wrong people. The solution can only be found if the governing bodies come together and find a schedule that allows players a chance to recover, rest, prepare and perform at certain junctions.

Yes, as part of that, the clubs have to also play their part, and there is nothing that I'm saying here I don't say to our ownership also. We all have a part to play if we want to fix this.

I wouldn't normally discuss a topic like this in a matchday programme, but I think today's occasion makes it pertinent. It's Liverpool v Everton, one of football's great fixtures, in one of the game's most historic competitions. I'm sure in the TV studios the discussion will be had about 'respecting the competition'. I ask anyone having those thoughts to look at the schedule, look at what all clubs have been asked to do in December and January, and ask: where is the respect for the players?

I can tell you without any uncertainty, the players and management of both clubs have nothing but respect for the FA Cup and value it deeply. It is a dream for all of us to win it. You'll see today from the commitment of both teams what it means – I have zero doubt.

I know both sides will give everything they have, because it means so much. It's for all of those involved in the running of the game – governing bodies, federations and yes, the clubs also – to come together and find a viable solution. It should not be on players and supporters to carry the burden.

Turning back to today, I welcome Carlo Ancelotti, his players, staff and supporters of Everton back to Anfield.

Carlo being back in the English game is so cool for the competitions and even cooler for Everton. I'm not sure if I'm doing either of us any favours by saying this, but in football terms I really do consider him a friend. Such an amazing person and just so generous in spirit and personality. He's won all there is to win, as a player and coach, and yet remains chilled and humble. He is a benchmark for those of us working in the game today on how to conduct yourself.

His impact at Everton is already being felt – we can see this from our analysis. He has been clever in picking up on the positivity of approach injected by Duncan Ferguson. Everton are always a difficult opponent for us because of the positive emotion they bring into this derby game. Under Carlo, with his experience, I think they have become even more dangerous.

But to be honest, I love this. I think it adds to the

occasion. My players have just as much desire and belief going into this game. We want to win it with all we have. We see the game as an opportunity. We know what our supporters expect. No Liverpool side can ever have less desire than the opponent – this is not allowed.

We go into this game today with complete confidence in our ability. We always focus on our own strengths while respecting the opponents. We will be on the front foot. We will channel the intensity to benefit our own approach. We will take all the positive energy this unique fixture brings.

Our supporters will know their importance also. There is no team-talk required for the Kop on days like this. They know their job. We will give all we have to make this an occasion to enjoy.

Liverpool 1, Everton 0

Goal: Jones (71)

Line-up (4-3-3): Adrian, Williams, Phillips, Gomez, Milner (c) (Larouci 9), Lallana, Chirivella, Jones, Elliott (Brewster 79), Minamino (Oxlade-Chamberlain 70), Origi. Subs not used: Kelleher, Mane, Henderson, Hoever

Jürgen's post-match reaction: 'Everybody asks me about Curtis Jones but there were so many extremely good performances. The goal was exceptional and the boy is an outstanding player. I like that the boys used all our patterns tonight to cause Everton problems. It was brilliant, absolutely brilliant.'

Saturday, January 11th, 5.30pm
Premier League
Tottenham 0, Liverpool 1

Goal: Firmino (37)

Line-up (4-3-3): Alisson, Alexander-Arnold, Gomez, Van Dijk, Robertson, Henderson (c), Wijnaldum, Oxlade-Chamberlain (Lallana 61), Firmino, Salah (Shaqiri 90+1), Mane (Origi 81). Subs not used: Adrian, Minamino, Phillips, Williams

Jürgen's post-match reaction [about having a record tally of 61 points after 21 games]: 'When somebody told me I didn't feel anything. I am in football for 50 years or so and if somebody would have told me that would ever happen I would probably have said it's not possible. Now it happened I don't feel [anything]. I don't know what is wrong with me, but it's really cool and exceptional. I told the boys what we should have done better, what we could have done better but I know if it would be easy to have that kind of winning streak then so many more teams would have done it. I can just say what we try to do with all we have is to create the basis for the rest of the season.'

Post-match notes

In winning 20 of their first 21 games, the Reds set the record for the best ever start to a top-flight season in Europe's top five leagues.

v Manchester United
Sunday, January 19th, 4.30pm

'JORDAN IS A SPECIAL PERSON, A SPECIAL PLAYER AND AN INCREDIBLE LEADER'

Premier League

GOOD afternoon and welcome back to Anfield for our Premier League fixture against Manchester United.

Firstly, I would like to welcome Ole Gunnar Solskjaer, his players, staff, officials and supporters of Manchester United for today's game. I am full of admiration for the work Ole is doing, this season in particular, given what he tries to juggle.

As a fellow manager it is easy to see the progress they make, although others on the outside are often not so quick to recognise.

They have recruited some exceptional players and the evolution of their squad makes them one of the strongest in Europe I would say.

Look at their talent from the keeper through to the forwards. They have world-class talent in that team and a squad full of match-winners. Big investment has resulted in a very strong group.

Of course, looking to build something takes time. We know this ourselves. But they build with outstanding results and performances as a foundation. Their win this week in the FA Cup against Wolves was yet more evidence of how dangerous they are.

United competes in four competitions still – this says a lot about their quality. They remain with much to fight for in the league, a semi-final second leg to come in the Carabao Cup, into the fourth round of the FA Cup and the knockout stages in Europe. You cannot compete as they do in these competitions if they are not an outstanding football team.

I have no idea how this contest has been billed externally but I also couldn't care less. I know how we have prepared and I know the respect we will show United.

I'm sure people will point to their brilliant win away against Manchester City. But we analyse far more – we look much deeper – and we know we face the most challenging of opponents today. If anyone thinks that win at City is the only signpost of danger, then they are silly and underestimating.

So far this season we have done well at getting the balance right in this regard. We respect the power of our opponent, but our main focus is always on us and our strengths and our qualities.

We know we are a very good football team. We know our players have the right values and approach. We believe in each other and what we do. We marry our belief with work, by which I mean it's important to always deliver quality yourself but respect that each fixture presents a new challenge.

The world around us constantly speaks of conclusions and outcomes. This is the world we live in, but we personally don't indulge in hypotheticals. We cannot afford to. Look beyond the next game before you play it and I promise you that the performance will suffer.

I am blessed with a dressing room that gets it. Most of you will see the interviews with our players and I'm sure there are a fair number who think: 'ah come on, of course they have to say this, but you believe differently.'

But I see it in them, this outstanding focus and attitude.

I don't just hear it. I saw it in the dressing room at Spurs.

We knew it was a big result, but we all knew all we had won was three points. To be honest, winning the three points is enough in these moments because it's the maximum we can win.

We also knew there were elements of the game that served as a warning for us. Warnings can be good if you treat them as lessons. So you see it, you learn from it, and you work to improve. That is what I saw in the away dressing room at Tottenham. A set of players who know the next performance needs to be better than the last. I love this.

Jordan Henderson is one of the many powerful voices on this. He'll be the first to tell you he's one of many – but he, as our captain, is so important.

I saw this week that he was voted the England men's team player of 2019. I was so pleased for him, because he deserves it. And as he said himself, that is an England set-up with some unbelievable players in it, who had a big year.

Jordan's commitment to club and country deserves

accolades like this. He's not big on individual awards and I know he often jokes that he's more accustomed to presenting them to team-mates than receiving them himself. But he's a special player, a special person and an incredible leader.

Turning back to today, I think Anfield knows how important it can be. Old Trafford undoubtedly helped United for the home game earlier in the season, but I'm confident our supporters can surpass that.

It's through our actions as a team that we can inspire them, but like the players, I expect our fans to come with the mindset that nothing short of our best will be good enough.

Anfield is at its best when the energy is positive and focused on our players. It's not animosity to the opponent that defines your importance as a supporter – it's your encouragement for us.

Our players run harder, jump higher and produce their best because of the positive energy you give to them. In those moments the shirts of the opposition team couldn't matter less.

The atmosphere should always be about joy. It should be about encouraging the team you are emotionally invested in. I always think the best occasions here are when we are all about us and what we do.

So let's all show our best face. The world is watching and we have a chance to show them that we define ourselves as a club by being together and by finding joy in the moment linked to our own actions.

Enjoy the game.

Liverpool 2, Manchester United 0

Goals: Van Dijk (14), Salah (90+3)

Line-up (4-3-3): Alisson, Alexander-Arnold, Gomez, Van Dijk, Robertson, Oxlade-Chamberlain (Lallana 66), Henderson (c), Wijnaldum, Salah, Firmino (Origi 83), Mane (Fabinho 83). Subs not used: Adrian, Minamino, Matip, Jones

Jürgen's post-match reaction: 'Good game, really good game. One of the best derbies we played for sure so far. Very dominant in most periods of the game. We played outstandingly well, we dominated the opponent, we played exactly in the space we had to. When we saw the line-up it was pretty clear what they wanted to do. The boys used the spaces really well, so dropping a six, being there, high full-backs, being flexible and creating a lot of chances. We scored from the set-piece but had other situations. And then the start of the second half was absolutely brutal – wow. We had, I don't know, three, four chances at least and didn't score. How it always is and how it often enough was now in that season, the opponent has the chance to come back. But we defend then with a lot of passion and big heart. [We were] carried as well by the atmosphere, which was great. Then the last situation in the game, Alisson Becker, what an assist and then Mo Salah, what a goal! There was a sprint duel of two really quick boys and Mo used his massive experience.'

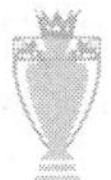

Thursday, January 23rd, 8pm
Premier League
Wolverhampton Wanderers 1, Liverpool 2

Goals: Henderson (8), Firmino (84)

Line-up (4-3-3): Alisson, Alexander-Arnold, Gomez, Van Dijk, Robertson, Henderson (c), Oxlade-Chamberlain (Fabinho 70), Wijnaldum, Salah (Origi 85), Firmino, Mane (Minamino 33). Subs not used: Adrian, Williams, Jones, Matip

Jürgen's post-match reaction: 'We knew this would be a really, really tough game. Wolves are doing so unbelievably well, they are so different to everything else you face during the year. How Nuno sets it up is just really good. That makes it difficult; the way they defend and then each ball you lose is 100 per cent a counter-attack but for that they had not too many chances. They scored a goal, a super goal, and had a really big one [chance] with an Ali save. I think we were four or five times in a one-on-one situation with the goalie, so there we could have scored. We scored a wonderful goal after a set-piece, but again not the second so everything is open and then it gets intense. They scored and then another five to 10 minutes, [it was] Wolves time. Mo again, Bobby alone in front of the goalie. Then a worldie from Bobby, a super, super, super goal. I think the two teams who played the most football so far played against each other, so nobody had an advantage. I am really, really pleased.'

Sunday, January 26, 5pm
FA Cup fourth round
Shrewsbury Town 2, Liverpool 2

Goals: Jones (15), Love (46og)

Line-up (4-3-3): Adrian, Williams, Matip (Salah 79), Lovren (c), Larouci, Fabinho, Chirivella, Jones, Minamino (Firmino 85), Elliott (Oxlade-Chamberlain 71), Origi. Subs not used: Kelleher, Keita, Hoever, Alexander-Arnold

Jürgen's post-match reaction: 'First and foremost, I have to say congratulations to Shrewsbury because it was well deserved. It was the minimum of what they deserved with the chances they had. Why they had the chances is because we lost the ball in the wrong moments and we played a few difficult passes which were difficult to control. We never got used to the pitch 100 per cent today. In the game, we scored a wonderful goal for 1-0 – really good football, a really nice goal – and then we got the present when they scored our second goal after half-time. But it didn't calm the game down or whatever, we conceded the penalty after losing the ball, a counter-attack and then it's a penalty. The second goal, we lose two challenges in a row and they finished the situation off brilliantly. That's it. The atmosphere over the 95 minutes was really good, but we brought Shrewsbury up and the crowd up with the way we played and that's what we have to admit. For us, not a wonderful football game.'

Wednesday, January 29th, 7.45pm
Premier League
West Ham United 0, Liverpool 2

Goals: Salah (35pen), Oxlade-Chamberlain (52)

Line-up (4-3-3): Alisson, Alexander-Arnold (Keita 77), Gomez, Van Dijk, Robertson, Henderson (c), Wijnaldum, Oxlade-Chamberlain (Jones 85), Origi (Fabinho 69), Salah, Firmino. Subs not used: Adrian, Lovren, Minamino, Matip

Jürgen's post-match reaction: 'I think the biggest chances we gave them. It was Gini's pass where we were alone in front of the goal and a sensational save from Ali, I think. Then Trent's post – slapstick situation, I don't know exactly how that happened. These situations, we gave pretty much away. These boys, I would give them my kids to take care of because I trust them 100 per cent, but in these situations they still can still make these kind of ridiculous mistakes. We had to face the challenge and the boys did it at the end with the help of a goalie who had nothing to do the whole night until he had to make world-class saves.'

Post-match notes

This was Jürgen Klopp's 50th away league win as Reds boss.

The win ensured the Reds had beaten every other team in the top flight in a single season for the first time.

FEB

2020

February 29th is a date that doesn't happen very often and in 2020 that day saw an event that doesn't happen very often – a Liverpool league defeat. Up until then the records had continued to tumble as Klopp's men looked every inch champions elect

1st: Southampton (PL) H
4th: Shrewsbury Town (FA) H
15th: Norwich City (PL) A
18th: Atletico Madrid (CL) A
24th: West Ham United (PL) H
29th: Watford (PL) A

v Southampton
Saturday, February 1st, 3pm

'MY PLAYERS HAVE BEEN ASKED A LOT OF QUESTIONS BUT THEY DON'T TIRE OF GIVING THE RIGHT ANSWERS'

Premier League

GOOD afternoon and welcome back to Anfield for our Premier League fixture against Southampton.

To begin with I would like to welcome Ralph Hasenhüttl, his players, staff, officials and supporters of our visitors to our home. Ralph is someone I have known about for some time before he came to England the season before, but in these moments now he is really showing football people in this country why he is so highly regarded across Europe.

Sensational leadership skills, bravery in decision-making and brilliant tactical knowledge. I think he rightly gets a lot of credit for how he has steered his team out of a difficult situation from the beginning of the season. But that is only part of the story. I can tell you from my own experiences, managing a team is often more about finding a way through the struggle than it is high-fives and hugs. You are presented with more problems to solve than you are with solutions.

In my career, as a manager, I learned more about myself in difficult times than I ever did in the good. The struggle is fulfilling when you do it with people you love and believe in.

This is why what Ralph has done, so far this campaign, will be admired so much by those of us who share his responsibilities and role.

Also, they have come through it while being adventurous and showing courage of approach. This

Southampton team plays great football and loves to attack you.

Today at Anfield we must be ready for a team that doesn't care about what position in the table either of us currently has.

They have international quality throughout and they play to their maximum. This makes them a dangerous opponent. And of course there is one player in their ranks we know better than most: Mr Danny Ings.

For 90-plus minutes today he is our opponent, but other than that he is always our friend at Liverpool. I am not even half-a-per-cent surprised to see what he does this season. Richly deserved, also.

I would never dream of telling Gareth Southgate what he should be considering, but given he is a top operator and clever coach, I'm sure he's aware that Danny is someone who could help his country again in the near future.

Today I hope he has an off-day, but other than that his story this season really brings joy to those of us lucky enough to know him.

Moving back to us, we have a very quick turnaround since our game on Wednesday in London. We knew this and we planned for it, but still we must now manage it.

The win against West Ham was very pleasing in how the boys managed the game. They will need to show the same qualities and then some more this afternoon.

Anfield has been an outstanding home for us so far this season, but it's been this way because we have all worked to make it so, players and supporters always together. For this to have a chance of continuing, so must the approach – and that means working harder and harder each time.

What defines us in this moment is the desire to always be better in the next game than we were in the last. I think after Wednesday we can do this.

The last fixture here on home soil was Manchester United and without question the energy from the crowd was decisive. It was as if the Kop willed Ali's ball and Mo's sprint and finish. I hope that is fresh in the mind of the Liverpool fans today. I hope they know that their contribution is what makes those moments possible.

After Wednesday I was asked whether I needed to find different ways to keep the players motivated. It was the easiest question I have been asked all season. An emphatic NO.

The motivation for these players is simply winning the next battle, be that a header or tackle, or a sprint, or a save or finish. They are motivated to win in each and every second of the game. And if you keep this mindset – win the moment that you are in – the rest takes care of itself.

Knowing how strong Southampton are in all departments is motivation today. Knowing we face an opponent who believes they can – and wants desperately to – beat us is motivation.

Knowing that in our dressing room we have a group of people who want to share amazing common experiences each time they present themselves is motivation.

My players have been asked a lot of questions so far this campaign but they don't tire of giving the right answers.

I love how they are their harshest critic and their own inspiration. Whatever the outcome today I am certain we will give all we have and do it for each other. This is all I can ever ask.

For the supporters and players, it's 3pm on a Saturday and Anfield is ready for us.

Knowing that is all the motivation we need.

Liverpool 4, Southampton 0

Goals: Oxlade-Chamberlain (47), Henderson (60), Salah (71, 90)

Line-up (4-3-3): Alisson, Alexander-Arnold, Gomez, Van Dijk, Robertson, Henderson (c) (Lallana 88), Fabinho, Wijnaldum (Minamino 81), Salah, Firmino, Oxlade-Chamberlain (Keita 73). Subs not used: Adrian, Lovren, Matip, Origi

Jürgen's post-match reaction: 'It's easy for me to use this game as a description for the situation. We have just incredibly difficult opponents to play against, they are not here to be part of any party, they want to hurt us normally – they want to beat us. That's absolutely normal. We have to throw everything we have on the pitch to get out of these games with a point or three points. And the boys do that, thankfully, and that's why we are where we are. But we don't take that for granted, not for a second. For today it was the best thing we could do. The attitude and the mentality of these boys made it again possible that we could win this game. Because this was a game which looked in moments not only tricky, it looked like – banana skin is maybe not the right word because Southampton are too good for being a banana skin – but it looked like today, yes it will probably happen [Liverpool would drop points]. The boys put a sensational shift in, everybody went to the point and above, so that makes this group really special. That's all that happened. We didn't want to have a 22-point difference to other teams today, we wanted to have 73 points after that matchday. And that's what we have, so all good for the moment. The boys have now a week off, we all have a week off, and then we go again. That's the only thing I know and all the rest we have to see. So many things can happen in football. Even when there's any decision made in the future, whenever that will be, why should we then stop thinking the same way? We have to use the skills of the boys, we have to use the character of the boys, we have to use the power of this club and especially of this stadium.'

Post-match notes

At the end of the day the Reds had a 22-point lead – the biggest gap between first and second ever in the top flight at the end of any day.

Tuesday, February 4th, 8pm
FA Cup fourth round replay
Liverpool 1, Shrewsbury Town 0

Goal: Williams (75og)

Line-up (4-3-3): Kelleher, Williams, Hoever, Van den Berg, Lewis, Chirivella (c), Clarkson (Dixon-Bonner 90+2), Cain, Elliott (Boyes 90+2), Jones, Millar (Hardy 82). Subs not used: Jaros, Gallacher, Bearne, Norris

Neil Critchley's post-match reaction: 'There was a message at half-time and at full-time [from Klopp]. There was a message before the game that Chelsea away could be an opportunity for one or two of them and they put in a performance tonight. James Milner trained with us yesterday and he asked whether he could come along. He was giving words of advice, he was getting right behind the players. He was vocal in the dressing room. He was animated. The boss is the boss. I'm only standing in for tonight and the players have done the club proud. The support we had was incredible, a full house – absolutely ridiculous.'

Post-match notes

With the first team on a winter break, Neil Critchley was manager for the night. James Milner was also in attendance to give his support from the sidelines as he continued his recovery from injury.

Saturday, February 15th, 5.30pm
Premier League
Norwich City 0, Liverpool 1

Goal: Mane (78)

Line-up (4-3-3): Alisson, Alexander-Arnold, Gomez, Van Dijk, Robertson, Wijnaldum (Fabinho 60), Henderson (c), Keita (Milner 84), Oxlade-Chamberlain (Mane 60), Salah, Firmino. Subs not used: Adrian, Lovren, Lallana, Origi

Jürgen's post-match reaction: 'It's easy to talk about the wind but on the pitch the boys have to deal with it. We played, for sure, two or three or four long balls too many. The formation was not prepared for that so we were not there for the second balls. We didn't obviously feel that we can play the balls through the smaller gaps. That was the wind but it would be still right. Our midfield was sometimes surprised by the long balls of our centre-halves and just couldn't push up early enough or quick enough, so we didn't win the second balls. You need to get used to circumstances and after 45 minutes we knew how it feels. More information from us at half-time and we could improve. We had so many counter-press situations where we won the ball back, where we put them under pressure, kept them under pressure and scored a wonderful goal. It helps when you have such quality on the bench to bring on. Sadio could have started today, of course, but I wanted to have a free decision for Tuesday.'

Tuesday, February 18th, 8pm
UEFA Champions League round of 16
Atletico Madrid 1, Liverpool 0

Line-up (4-3-3): Alisson, Alexander-Arnold, Gomez, Van Dijk, Robertson, Fabinho, Henderson (c) (Milner 80), Wijnaldum, Mane (Origi 45), Salah (Oxlade-Chamberlain 72), Firmino. Subs not used: Adrian, Keita, Minamino, Matip

Jürgen's post-match reaction: 'I have no problem with the result. I am not disappointed about how we played, I saw much worse games in my life. It was absolutely okay. We were not good enough in the last third, that's it. I didn't expect that we would have around about 70 per cent possession. I actually thought we would have a little bit more of the game, but we are not surprised. 1-0 and you are not in the best moment, you try to defend it with all you have and that's what they did. That's absolutely okay, I respect that a lot, but of course it is only 1-0. We are not 5-0 down or whatever. We think we have a chance, we don't think it will be easy, not at all because Atletico will probably have back Joao Felix, Diego Costa in different circumstances and we have to see who we can line up with because a lot can happen until then because there are a lot of games. But, as long as we can get 11 players in a Liverpool shirt, we will try it with all we have. For all Atletico fans who can get a ticket for the game, welcome to Anfield.'

v West Ham United
Monday, February 24th, 8pm

'THIS IS A GOOD TIME TO SHOW THE HUNGER WE HAVE TO ACHIEVE THINGS AT THE END OF THE SEASON'

Premier League

GOOD evening and welcome back to Anfield for our match against West Ham United.

I start by offering a warm return to David Moyes – someone who knows the city of Liverpool really well.

It feels like quite a long time ago now that he was in charge of our close neighbours Everton, but I am sure he still has many close friends in this area.

He is, of course, one of the most respected managers in the English game and has a tried and tested way of working that has always served him and the clubs he worked for well.

Even though I am certain David considers Liverpool a big rival personally because of the battles he had while with Everton and then Manchester United, he is also someone who I know was a big supporter of the Hillsborough families during their struggles and for that he will always have the deepest of respect here.

As well as David, I welcome the West Ham players, staff, officials and supporters to our home.

We played each other not so long ago and it was already apparent David and his guys are making an impact on making them more competitive. That was a really tough game – like so many this campaign – and we were made to work for every inch.

It will be exactly the same again tonight – if not more difficult. You look in their dressing room and you see characters who will relish the chance to come here and get a positive result. They have the quality to do so – they have the strength to do so – and all this means they have the opportunity to do so. This means we must be ready.

Like all of us in this amazingly competitive league, West Ham are in a position where every point is precious. Same for us. And with every point being precious it means the matches will be fiercely contested. Again, we must be ready.

But West Ham's need and desire isn't any less or more than ours. We have exactly the same approach in terms of knowing the importance of being ready to give everything to achieve the objective.

On our side, we are so lucky to have the players who embrace the mentality and attitude we need in moments like this.

Respect the opponent. Prepare on the basis that nothing less than everything will be enough. Then go into the game focusing on your own qualities and believing in your own ability to get the job done.

It's the first time back at Anfield for the senior team in what feels like a while, because of the mid-season break and then successive away matches in the Premier League and Champions League.

I must say it's fantastic to be back. We come into this after contrasting results – having won at Norwich by a single goal and lost in Madrid by the identical margin.

In many ways both those games and both those results illustrate how hard we have to keep working if we want to achieve things. It didn't feel to us that we played worse in the game we lost – maybe at times we played better. But at the level we live at now, games are close and so competitive, the line between being in a dressing room with the result you want and the opposite feeling is very narrow.

I could not fault for a second the attitude and application of the team in Madrid last Tuesday. The intensity of our performance was really pleasing and I told that to the boys.

There was nothing from last week that should set us back. We should look at it the other way. An opportunity to immediately strike back. We have a talented opponent coming to our home and they want to leave with the win. This is enough motivation.

I will be happy if we take this approach into the match tonight. We'll need to be at our very best, we know that.

What will be critical for us this evening is the support from our greatest asset of all – the Anfield crowd.

It's a Monday night and it's under the lights. It's been a break since we were all here last and I think that adds to the hunger.

But most important is that our supporters recognise just how much we need them.

They have played a huge role in giving us the base

we have currently. Now – like the players – it's about upping the game for the decisive period. Anfield will be ready to perform, as they and the team have done until now, to the highest level imaginable.

Tonight is a good time I think to show the hunger we have collectively to achieve things at the end of this season. We all recognise there is work to do – lots of work to do. We can only affect and impact the next game. Therefore everyone who loves Liverpool inside the ground tonight should make sure we give everything we have for this fixture.

Liverpool 3, West Ham 2

Goals: Wijnaldum (9), Salah (68), Mane (81)

Line-up (4-3-3): Alisson, Alexander-Arnold, Gomez, Van Dijk (c), Robertson, Keita (Oxlade-Chamberlain 57), Fabinho, Wijnaldum, Salah, Firmino, Mane (Matip 90+1). Subs not used: Adrian, Lovren, Minamino, Lallana, Origi

Jürgen's post-match reaction [including his thought on equalling the top-flight records for consecutive home league wins and consecutive wins]: 'A couple of years ago, three or four, maybe in the beginning, I said we want to write our own stories, we want to create our own history. Obviously, the boys took really seriously what I said there and that's all cool – but just not too important in the moment. It's so special, the numbers are incredible, so difficult. We said it a couple of times, we spoke about wonderful games, brilliant games, we spoke about hard games, difficult games. Tonight was difficult obviously, so the number of wins you can only have if you win all of these games: the difficult ones, the easy ones – if there ever was one – the brilliant ones and the rougher, more grumpy ones. In the end, that's what counts. We all know it's very special, but in the moment we are really just in the situation and want to recover and prepare for the next one. The next opponent is really waiting and wants to fight us, the whole stadium at Watford will go for us, that's completely normal. I saw the boys tonight, they are ready to fight, but we still have a lot of work to do. The crowd was really helpful, we had a lot of set-pieces, Ox came on, we changed the set-pieces slightly, we had these crosses. The crosses were a bit too hard from time to time, it's easy to say but much more difficult to change. I really thought the positioning was brilliant but in the end the crosses looked like shots. But we scored the two goals. Our third goal was really good, you have to react on balls like this, a deflected ball. Our second goal was really good play but of course unlucky for West Ham in the way it went in. The best goal we scored was the disallowed one, I liked it a lot, it was exactly the way we wanted to play. We brought it over the line. It was difficult, we knew it before. West Ham were much better than they were against us in the first game.'

Post-match notes

Klopp's men equalled the all-time English top-flight records for consecutive home wins (21) and successive victories (18).

Saturday, February 29th, 5.30pm
Premier League
Watford 3, Liverpool 0

Line-up (4-3-3): Alisson, Alexander-Arnold, Lovren, Van Dijk (c), Robertson, Fabinho, Wijnaldum (Lallana 61), Oxlade-Chamberlain (Origi 65), Mane, Salah, Firmino (Minamino 79). Subs not used: Adrian, Matip, Jones, Hoever

Jürgen's post-match reaction: 'I am not surprised by the performance because it would mean I have never seen something like that before – and I have seen it a lot of times. So, what I can say, I think 3-0 is a bit harsh but we had a big hand in that. We have to start with the most important thing and that is to congratulate Watford. We didn't perform like we should have and Watford performed exactly how they wanted. The first two goals were completely different – one is a throw-in, a bouncing ball, Troy [Deeney] used his body again in that situation, so we cannot defend that ball. The second one, we lose the ball, they pass the ball and Sarr is on his bike and scores a really nice one. The third one we gave away pretty much by ourselves, but in the end it was still a nice finish from Troy Deeney. We had not enough chances, we didn't create enough and that's what leads then to defeat. We have to admit Watford were the better team.'

Post-match notes

Losing to Watford brought to an end a 44-game unbeaten run in the Premier League, stretching back to January 2019.

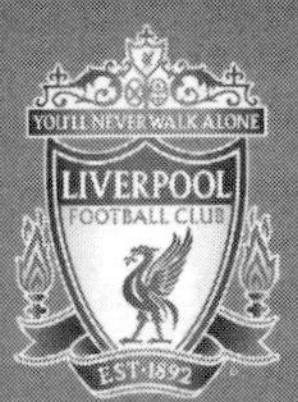

MAR

2020

Klopp's dreams of leading the Reds to a third successive Champions League final were dashed and the club's FA Cup run came to a halt but a 25-point lead at the top of the Premier League table had turned league title doubters into believers. Then the season took a dramatic turn...

3rd: Chelsea (FA) A
7th: Bournemouth (PL) H
11th: Atletico Madrid (CL) H

Tuesday, March 3rd, 7.45pm
FA Cup fifth round
Chelsea 2, Liverpool 0

Line-up (4-3-3): Adrian, Williams, Gomez, Van Dijk (c), Robertson, Fabinho, Lallana (Salah 80), Jones (Milner 70), Minamino, Mane, Origi (Firmino 70). Subs not used: Lonergan, Oxlade-Chamberlain, Matip, Chirivella

Jürgen's post-match reaction: 'Losing 2-0 is not cool, but in this case it is relatively easy to explain – we made two massive mistakes around the goals. Adrian made a super save a second or two seconds before and then this ball, a really good shot from Willian and he could not make that save. But before that we lost the ball and that's a problem. It was not the biggest shock because it is football. I liked the reaction, liked the way we played, some good stuff, it was a super-intense game and both teams were really running like mad. It was clear it would be difficult, but we had our moments, we had good chances, especially the one where I don't know who saved the balls – a defender or the goalie or whatever – when we shot three or four times. We conceded a second one and that didn't help obviously and it was then a bit more difficult to take. Chelsea defended with all they had, threw the bodies in, really physical. We couldn't score, they couldn't score and so the game finished 2-0 and we are out of the competition, which is the opposite of what we wanted.'

v Bournemouth
Saturday, March 7th, 12.30pm

'WE HAVE HAD COUNTLESS SETBACKS BUT WE'VE ALWAYS FOUND THE ANSWER'

Premier League

GOOD afternoon and welcome back to Anfield for our Premier League game against Bournemouth.

I guess the first place to start is to admit our last two results haven't been good enough, and particularly our performance at Watford last weekend.

There is no hiding from the fact we were disappointed by the outcomes of both games in the last week and rightly so.

Because of our good run this season, and in fact into last season too, perhaps our last two games have been a bigger topic of discussion that they would be normally. I understand this and I am absolutely okay with it.

But internally I can tell you it has been business as usual. As always, we have had our analysis meetings, looked at where we were not good enough, then we've trained hard and prepared ourselves to fight once again.

We never hide from truths here, it is one of our strengths. We know we have done extremely well to get into the amazing position we find ourselves in. We were not carried here – we had to fight and battle our way here.

What this group of players have done, until now, for me is sensational. I am so proud of them and I am so appreciative of them.

Truthfully, both my coaches and I could not feel more blessed than to have this incredible group of people to work with each and every day.

And the main reason why they are so good – world-class good – is because they are completely honest. Honest with themselves and honest with us, always.

It's this professional and intellectual honesty that defines them in many ways. They have no harsher critic than themselves. As the person privileged to lead them, I don't have to worry about the mindset or mentality.

The job in this moment is to look at the practical issues, the problems we have encountered in recent games, and fix them.

It really is that simple. It's our job and our life at this level.

I think I have spoken in these pages before that one of the myths of this season is that we have avoided setbacks. We have had countless setbacks but we have always found the answer. That's what these boys do. They see opportunity in every moment – it's a wonderful trait of theirs.

Today is one of those opportunities. We know there will be added focus on us because of recent weeks. Good – no problem for us or this team. It is good that today we face one of the hungriest and most determined opponents possible. This means there can only be proper focus. Nothing else will be good enough.

I welcome Eddie Howe, his players, staff, officials and supporters of Bournemouth to Anfield.

I have often written in here what I think of Eddie,

so no need to be repetitive. Quite simply he is one of the best out there. But I can add that this season my admiration has grown even greater.

I wrote earlier about responding to problems. Wow, how they deal with their issues this season and still fight and win is incredible. It really is. And as always with Eddie and his guys, they fight while remaining true to their principles.

This is why he will always be admired so much by his fellow managers.

Bournemouth arrive here knowing there is big opportunity for them. This is fine for us, because we know what we face. A very talented opponent – highest motivation possible and with belief. Tough job.

We know a number of the players within their ranks also. Harry Wilson is still 'ours' so cannot play today – this is good news for us, I would say. We have all been delighted to see Harry's progress and growth. Super boy and a super player.

Also, Dom Solanke and Jordon Ibe are players I was fortunate to work with here. Love them both as people and players. Both having fantastic careers and will continue to do so. As long as they're not playing against us in a specific game I always wish them well.

I love that today will be as difficult as any game we have here this season because of all the circumstances. It's a challenge, it's a fight, it's a battle, it's a problem.

But there is also a solution and we have that within our power.

And when I say 'we' I really mean the power of the Liverpool collective. Players and supporters. Today it is so, so, so important.

It's an early kick-off, there is an external mood around us, so the challenge is there. When we – collectively – have faced challenges in recent years we have come together to meet them.

Players know they must inspire the fans, but our supporters know they can also influence what happens on the pitch. It's coolest when both do it in unison. We have been fortunate it happens most of the time.

My team-talk today for anyone with a Liverpool heart beating in their chest is forget any other game, any other occasion, any other issue. Be in the moment today. Be there for this team and be there for each other. Today is our first, last and everything football-wise. Let's enjoy every second of it.

I can tell those supporters who were in the stadium with us at Watford and Chelsea, we heard you. We heard you singing for us at the end, despite how disappointed you may have been, and we appreciated it, as we always do.

Your support is one of the key reasons why we've been able to have the season we have had so far, so let's do it again today.

Liverpool 2, Bournemouth 1

Goals: Salah (24), Mane (33)

Line-up (4-3-3): Adrian, Alexander-Arnold, Gomez, Van Dijk, Milner (c), Oxlade-Chamberlain (Lallana 84), Fabinho, Wijnaldum, Salah, Firmino (Origi 90+2), Mane. Subs not used: Lonergan, Keita, Minamino, Matip, Williams

Jürgen's post-match reaction: 'I was absolutely happy about the result, the three points and the performance because I knew it would be tricky for different reasons. I think the decisions of the ref around the goals made it even more tricky for us, obviously. We wanted to fight back before the game and after that we had to fight back. How we played after being 1-0 down was exceptional, to be honest. I don't want to make it too big but in a moment when you have to fight back for the momentum and then you get a decision like that and a goal like this, there are other teams in the history of football which would then slip. The boys' reaction today, I loved – I really loved. We fought hard, played super football, the strikers played really well together and were connected. We had good passing behind, we had two super situations [with a] pass from half-space; one for Mo from Millie, I think, and one probably Ox for Trent where we could have scored more goals. We didn't score then, that's okay. Second half, we controlled the game. But the biggest chance in the second half was obviously Fraser's. Millie saved our life but I really think we deserved that today. We had moments but didn't finish it off. But the attitude again, the reaction to the different knocks, I liked a lot. So after the final whistle I was really happy.'

v Atletico Madrid
Wednesday, March 11th, 8pm

'EVERYTHING THIS GROUP HAS THEY HAVE FOUGHT FOR. WE ARE FIGHTERS TO OUR VERY CORE'

UEFA Champions League round of 16

GOOD evening and welcome back to Anfield for our UEFA Champions League match against Atletico Madrid.

What can I say about this game other than it's as tough a challenge as there is. This is what it is all about. What a game in prospect, what a battle, what a contest.

I welcome Diego Simeone, his players, staff, officials and the supporters of our visitors to Anfield tonight.

I spoke at length before the first tie about my personal admiration for Mr Simeone. He is a remarkable leader who has done a remarkable job over many years. He is regarded as one of Europe's elite coaching talents and it is not hard to see why.

He has made Atletico into a team and club that reflects his own image. They have had great success already under his leadership and it is clear they are set up for success again in the future.

This current Atletico team is exceptional, as we found out in Madrid not too long ago. They have all the tools to be the best team in Europe. From back to front: world-class players with a winners mentality. World-class leadership in the dugout. This is a good combination if you are someone who supports Atletico.

They arrive here in the lead this evening and we cannot and do not ignore this fact. A big part of what we are, as a team, is that we are humble enough to acknowledge the strengths of our opponents at all times.

It is unavoidable to recognise that one of our visitors' big qualities is the ability to defend something they already have. Arguably they are the world's best at it – in all sporting disciplines. But we don't look on this fact as daunting. No, the opposite. What a fantastic challenge.

Really – what an opportunity! We love to be tested. We love to pit ourselves against the very best.

The story of our team in recent seasons, and even in recent months and weeks, is when we face a challenge we rise to it. Set the bar higher and give all you have to clear it.

Our mentality isn't one whereby we expect or want gifts. Everything this group of players has in this moment they have fought and scrapped for. We are fighters to our very core. Opportunity is the pressure that drives us – it is only positive in these moments.

I talk about Atletico's qualities because we must respect them, but in doing so we don't ignore our own. This is so, so important.

We have talent, desire, energy and belief. We know when we bring our intensity we hold the pen and we write the story. We have world-class players, who I am proud to say are world-class people also. I would swap them for no-one.

But the key part of that is knowing there is work to do and we have to do it. It is not allowed to think for even a second our previous achievements will have an impact tonight. Things happen when you make them happen – tonight we have to make them happen.

Just because we have done something before doesn't mean you can expect it to happen again. Go and make it happen again – performance and atmosphere.

Anyone who comes to Anfield tonight thinking of previous occasions and feelings here, I'm cool with that. But it has to be channelled into a mindset of 'I want to feel it again'.

So, remember all the things that brought you to that feeling – player and supporter.

The key word tonight will be 'intensity'. Madrid will have it – we know this. So we must have higher intensity, in the positive sense, in all that we do.

Our visitors' supporters will be passionate and loud. Cool! We can be better if we are prepared to work for it. Our visitors' players will be focused, prepared and hungry. Cool! We can be better if we are prepared to work for it.

I cannot emphasise enough how important it is to leave any sense of 'what if' or even 'what might be' outside the stadium. In the stands and on the pitch we need to be in every moment.

This is how you create special moments.

Wanting something isn't enough. Plenty will want something.

We have proved already, and we can prove again,

it's about 'doing'. It's about doing the work and then getting the rewards.

Anfield has been our biggest asset for such a long time and we never fall into the trap of thinking it just happens because tickets are sold and gates are opened.

On nights like this, the Anfield crowd is the 'transfer' that no other club can ever acquire, no matter how much they crave it. It can't be copied or replicated. It's special to us. It is ours and we must always cherish its positive impact.

As always the message to the players and the crowd is very similar. Be yourselves, trust yourselves, embrace the joy of the moment and do your best.

It's all you can ever ask.

Liverpool 2, Atletico Madrid 3
(Atletico Madrid win 4-2 on aggregate)

Goals: Wijnaldum (43), Firmino (94)

Line-up (4-3-3): Adrian, Alexander-Arnold, Gomez, Van Dijk, Robertson, Oxlade-Chamberlain (Milner 82), Henderson (c) (Fabinho 105), Wijnaldum (Origi 105), Salah, Firmino (Minamino 113), Mane. Subs not used: Lonergan, Lallana, Matip

Jürgen's post-match reaction: 'I think everybody who saw the game tonight knows that it could have been different. I loved our first 90 or 95 minutes, however long it was. Our first, main mistake tonight was that we scored the second goal too late; we scored in extra-time and not in the 90 minutes, so that was our fault. When you see a team like Atletico packed with world-class players in their positions and they play the way they play, it is the most difficult thing to do, to face, that's how it is. We did exceptionally well, we played exactly in the spaces we have to play. I loved the football we played, I loved how we played in the half-spaces, I loved how we used our triangles, squares on the left and right side, how we passed the ball, how we came to finishes. We wanted to have first-touch crosses and we had [them], it's how we scored the first goal – a super goal. We caused them more problems than probably people thought after the first game; against a defensive set-up like that, to cause a team that many problems is really exceptional, so I loved that. But we scored the second goal, all good and then everybody saw their first goal. Come on, if you lose – and we lost tonight – you do it always for some reason and they're always different. Tonight, of course, that pass was not really helpful. Adrian is a super player, I love the boy, but it is in this moment the wrong decision, or he didn't hit the ball right. In this moment the momentum changed. Before that, Madrid thought, 'Wow, how should we cope with that?' In that moment, everything that was natural before that – how we played, how we were positioned, what we did – it was not easy, but it felt natural [and] right. But it changed and was now different and they were now, 'Ah, okay, could be our game tonight', so we became a bit stiff and they became a little bit fresher legs or whatever. In the end they scored two more goals and we didn't, so we lost both games – congratulations to Atletico, they are through.'

Following the Atletico Madrid match the growing global threat of the coronavirus led to the postponing of the remainder of the football season. In a worrying time, Jürgen Klopp was a measured voice who put football into perspective. His comments drew praise from the World Health Organisation

‘FOOTBALL ALWAYS SEEMS THE MOST IMPORTANT OF THE LEAST IMPORTANT THINGS. TODAY FOOTBALL AND FOOTBALL MATCHES AREN’T IMPORTANT AT ALL’

I DON'T think this is a moment where the thoughts of a football manager should be important, but I understand for our supporters they will want to hear from the team and I will front that.

First and foremost, all of us have to do whatever we can to protect one another. In society I mean. This should be the case all the time in life, but in this moment I think it matters more than ever.

I've said before that football always seems the most important of the least important things. Today, football and football matches really aren't important at all.

Of course, we don't want to play in front of an empty stadium and we don't want games or competitions suspended, but if doing so helps one individual stay healthy – just one – we do it no questions asked.

If it's a choice between football and the good of the wider society, it's no contest. Really, it isn't.

Today's decision and announcement is being implemented with the motive of keeping people safe. Because of that we support it completely. We have seen members of teams we compete against become ill. This virus has shown that being involved in football offers no immunity. To our rival clubs and individuals who are affected and to those who later will become so, you are in our thoughts and prayers.

None of us know in this moment what the final outcome will be, but as a team we have to have belief that the authorities make decisions based on sound judgement and morality.

Yes, I am the manager of this team and club and therefore carry a leadership responsibility with regards to our future on the pitch. But I think in the present moment, with so many people around our city, the region, the country and the world facing anxiety and uncertainty, it would be entirely wrong to speak about anything other than advising people to follow expert advice and look after themselves and each other.

The message from the team to our supporters is only about your well-being. Put your health first. Don't take any risk. Think about the vulnerable in our society and act where possible with compassion for them.

Please look after yourselves and look out for each other.

You'll Never Walk Alone,

Jürgen

LOCKDOWN MEMORIES

While football took a break, Jürgen could take stock, plan the next steps and even let people know how he was spending his new-found leisure time

On coping with being locked down...

It is a difficult time for all of us, but from a personal point of view an interesting one as well because I've never had a situation like this and was never that long at home. From a personal point of view, I am really good, but like everybody else, [I am] concerned about the situation around us, of course.

On what happened just before everyone was sent home...

It feels like it is ages ago that we played Atletico and Thursday was a day off. I remember, we all knew about the situation with coronavirus around the world but we were still 'in our tunnel', if you want, and until then it didn't really arrive into our mind in England. We played the Bournemouth game on Saturday, we won it, then Sunday City lost, so the information for us was 'two wins to go'. But then on Monday morning, I woke up and heard about the situation in Madrid, that they would close the schools and universities from Wednesday, so it was really strange to prepare for that game, to be honest. I usually don't struggle with things around me, I can build barriers right and left when I prepare for a game, but in that moment it was really difficult. Wednesday we had the game, I loved the game, I loved what I saw from the boys, it was a really, really good performance other than the result – we didn't score enough, we conceded too many, that's all clear, but between these two main pieces of information it was a brilliant game! Thursday [we were] off and then Friday when we arrived it was already clear this is not a session. Yes, we trained, but it was more of a meeting. We had a lot of things to talk about, a lot of things to think about, things I never thought before in my life about. Nobody knew exactly – and nobody knows exactly – how it will go on, so the only way we could do it was to organise it as good as possible for the boys and make sure everything is sorted as much as we can sort it in our little space, in the little area where we are responsible, really. That's what we did in a very short time, then we sent the boys home, went home ourselves and here we are still.

On his parting words to the players...
Usually I understand much more about the things I am talking about, to be honest! How could I explain the situation around corona? No chance. Look, in my job, in my life, I face a lot of problems – completely different problems to the ones we have now, but problems anyway – and I am a completely solution-orientated person. I am not really interested in the problem usually; I take it as information and I immediately work on the solutions. In this case, no chance; for me, no chance; for anybody, [no chance] in the short term. It will all be sorted and we know that, but not in the short term. So, what could I really know about? I had the same amount

of questions like the boys, [that] I couldn't answer – but we did, meanwhile. We spoke a couple of times, we have a really intense, big, big group chat – the whole of Melwood are in that. The boys are really lively in that, the boys are just interested in what everybody is doing, comments on what everybody is doing – if Ox is on Instagram or whatever! So, that helps a lot. The mood is good. As I said, it is a challenge for all of the people as we know [and] we know that our life is still good. There are so many people out there that have much bigger problems so it would feel really embarrassing to myself if I was to talk about my 'problems' – I have the problems every person in the world has in the moment. That's the lesson we learn in this moment. Four or five weeks ago it looks like a lot of countries thought, 'That's our problem, that's our problem, that's our problem, we have a problem with them' and stuff like this. Now nature shows us we are all the same and we have all the same problems in the same moment, and we have to work together on the solution. There is nothing good in that situation apart from maybe what we can learn from that.

On his admiration for key workers during the pandemic...

My English is not good enough to say. It's extraordinary, it's great. I was sent a video of people in the hospital just outside the intensive care area and when they started singing 'You'll Never Walk Alone' I started crying immediately. It's unbelievable. But it shows everything, these people not only work but they have such a good spirit. They are used to helping other people, we need to get used to it because usually we have our own problems and stuff. But it's their job, they do it day in and day out. They bring themselves, if you want, in danger because they help ill, sick and seriously handicapped people, so I couldn't admire them more and appreciate it more.

On how his team adapted to their situation…

First and foremost, I have to say – not only the backroom staff, I miss everybody. I just miss everybody. It's two weeks and I'm not on holiday. Usually you are somewhere and that's not a moment where you miss the backroom staff or your colleagues. But at the moment, really desperately. We miss each other, we really like working together. We have a lot of contact with WhatsApp groups and phone calls, FaceTime, whatever. So we see each other a lot but not like we want to or like we are used to, but they still do an incredible job. Look, yes, we all have the same problems but there are some special problems on top of that. We have the players and it's difficult for football players, like it's difficult for me, to go normal shopping, food shopping. We have to do social distancing and we try that. We are now in the second week at home. We respect absolutely 100 per cent the situation and want to play our part in it.

On his players' appearances on social media...

I didn't cut the grass [like James Milner] but I tried the dance of Ox! Not as bad as you probably think! It's very important in these times that we all show we take this situation seriously, but we are human beings. At the moment we are at home and when you are at home, you cannot do something to help outside. We are not health workers, we don't work in a supermarket. You have to keep your own mood up and you have to keep the mood up for other people. If the boys do anything on Instagram, as long as it's in a legal frame I'm overly happy about it – it just shows they are still cheeky and all that stuff. I like it, I like it a lot. I like the line-ups they do. All these things are really funny. It's good.

On his players' online training sessions...

It's just great. Look, it's so different. Everything is different in the moment and we do all different stuff. When we have these training sessions, I could have never imagined I would enjoy it that much but it's just the moment when I see the boys again and that changes everything – for a minute, for an hour, for two hours, however long the sessions are. The boys are all in good spirits; you feel immediately why you miss them so much, because it's just an exceptional group. You want to be together with them, you want to have them around, you want to be closer to them than you can be. These are the closest moments, apart from exchanging messages with them and asking, 'How are you?' and stuff like this. So I enjoy these sessions really a lot.

On what he watched on TV during lockdown…

We watched 'Downton Abbey', which I really like. We only watch television in the evening, but what can you do apart from playing games and stuff like that? We watch quite a few things. Last night I watched, until late, 'Icarus' – very interesting. Meanwhile, I never watched Marvel movies. I saw now 'Ironman' and stuff like this, which I enjoyed as well. You don't have to think a lot. This kind of stuff, just entertainment because I cannot watch the news all day.

On learning new life skills…

I'm now in charge of dishwashing, which is nice actually. I enjoy it. I'm master of that little machine now. And I did my first scrambled eggs. Nothing else since then because Ulla was impressed about the scrambled eggs but didn't want to give me another opportunity since then, I didn't really ask for it. But the challenge for next week is I'm 52 now and I cannot tie a tie. After this week I should be able to tie a tie. It will probably take a full week because my hands are completely useless usually, so it will be funny.

On his first day back at Melwood…

I woke up even earlier than usual, and then I realised

it is my first day. It felt like the first day at school; for me, it was 46 years ago, but it must have been similar. I dressed myself in my uniform again – and for the right reason, for going to training. I drove to Melwood and was really happy to see all the boys. We are ready to go and it was really nice to be back.

On returning to football being like pre-season…

It will not be the same as other pre-seasons. But, yes, it's a pre-season. Usually our players have two or three weeks' holiday a year, now they had nine weeks off. It was not a holiday but it was nine weeks off. That's good from one point of view – finally they got a real rest. On the other side, of course, you cannot rest when you are worried about the situation in the world, not in the same way like you do on a proper holiday.

On the motivation to become champions…

For me, it [last season] was not a disappointment. They [Manchester City] won it, we didn't win it – done. We won the Champions League final – great. Let's carry on. The more important information for me was how good we can be; if we are really concentrated, if we are really focused, and if we improve a couple of things we can get even better. If you are a really good football team then you have to win football games, so now it's about us to decide how many football games we will win. We really take it game by game.

JUN

2020

More than three months after their last competitive action, Jürgen's men were readied for a big return. They faced two tricky opponents in eerie, empty stadiums but workrate and wonderful football put a talented squad on the verge of their ultimate goal...

21st: Everton (PL) A
24th: Crystal Palace (PL) H

Sunday, June 21st, 7pm
Premier League
Everton 0, Liverpool 0

Line-up (4-3-3): Alisson, Alexander-Arnold, Matip (Lovren 73), Van Dijk, Milner (Gomez 42), Fabinho, Henderson (c), Keita (Wijnaldum 65), Minamino (Oxlade-Chamberlain 45), Firmino (Origi 65), Mane. Subs not used: Adrian, Salah, Elliott, Williams

Jürgen's post-match reaction: 'The point is the one we deserved, even when I have to admit that, of course, Everton had the biggest chance to win the game. That was a little bit our problem, that we didn't create enough chances with all the possession we had. I liked the intensity level of the game, I liked the high-press, counter-press, all these kind of things. I didn't like too much – but you cannot force that – the rhythm. We had good football moments absolutely, not until the last moment, the decisive moment where you have a free shot of whatever. We didn't have enough chances for sure, but that's how it is. When I think about it, I think all the derbies here at Goodison looked pretty similar honestly. I think the result is similar. At Anfield, the games are most of the time slightly better. Here at Goodison it was always like this – two teams, aggressive, very physical. Everton [were well] organised, so we had to run a lot, which I like. It looked good, we looked fit, we looked ready. I know we can play better football but the performance level was okay.'

v Crystal Palace
Wednesday, June 24th, 8.15pm

'THE PASSION SO MANY FEEL FOR THE GAME WILL BRING JOY TO MANY WHEN WE REALLY NEED IT'

Premier League

HELLO and my best wishes to you wherever you are in this moment.

I always begin my programme column with "Welcome to Anfield" for the game, but of course for the time being we live in different times. But still, I extend my best wishes to all of you and I do welcome Crystal Palace, Roy Hodgson, his players, staff and officials to our home for this Premier League fixture.

My respect for Roy and how he leads his club has never been higher and the season they have shows they continue to progress under his leadership. A brilliant squad of players, superbly organised and a massive threat, so we look forward to the challenge of facing them and know it will be tough.

But it's really hard to even know where to start with these words, when talking about the circumstances we face.

It is important to begin by saying I hope you and your loved ones are healthy and safe. Unfortunately because of the nature of the terrible virus there will be those of you reading this who have lost family members or close friends during this period. I doubt very much there is a person on the planet who doesn't have a connection to someone who has been affected by the tragic consequences of what we have collectively been through and continue to face.

I say many times when asked about topics which aren't

football-related and therefore my area of knowledge, that I feel woefully under-qualified to speak on it. But it is clear we were all impacted and we all had experiences since March which will live with us forever.

Not for one second would I diminish the pain and trauma this awful pandemic has caused, but I am by nature a positive person and therefore I have sought where possible to seek the positives, no matter how well-hidden they are.

The biggest positive, in my view, is that this global catastrophe taught us actually how much we need each other and that our first instincts should be to help and care for those around us who need it the most.

We all hate that this thing has happened, but I am filled with hope for our future because I think as a society, across the world, we showed our best face. Ignore for one moment the politicians and their decisions and think about how we reacted as people. We were responsible, we showed appreciation for the heroes who risked their lives for us, we learned, we connected, we cared and we realised that love is a more powerful motivator than fear.

And this does link to football and what we do, because I totally understand that when there was talk of the Premier League coming back, for many people it did not sit well. I get this 100 per cent. But we cannot ignore the positive impact that our game has on millions upon millions and that returning to play means we have a chance, as a community, for collective experiences again.

Yes, for the future of the industry and for the clubs themselves, returning was critical. No one made a more compelling case for this than the chairman of our opponent today, Crystal Palace. I read his article and at the time he was swimming against the tide of opinion, so it was as brave as it was smartly articulated. Mr Steve Parish did as good a job as anyone in explaining the importance of working to safeguard the future of the professional game at our level and I think he deserves great credit for this.

Aside from the important discussion around that, there is the emotional uplift we will hopefully see in the coming weeks as our season concludes. Not for one second am I saying that the return of Premier League football will offer comfort to those who have suffered the worst possible loss – I am not silly enough to think this. But the passion so many feel for the game and the clubs they follow will bring joy to many at a time when we really need it.

Yes, we have still many challenges. You will not find a single player, coach, official or supporter who prefers football in empty stadiums to full ones. However, we should also remember how we all first fell in love with this game and I am confident to guess for the majority it was playing it. No one ever played their first football match in front of a crowd and yet the love-affair began during those moments.

No one will miss supporters inside Anfield more than me, I promise, but the situation is the situation, so we learn from the positive experience of this pandemic and we make the best of it. Those of you reading this now, who will no doubt be watching the match today, you are still with us. If you watch with your entire household or you watch by yourself because of the circumstances, you are with us today.

We know what our club and this group of players in particular means to you. We know the joy it brings. We know you kick every ball and shout still as if you were in the middle of the Kop. We know the impact of what we do now will be as big as anything we have ever done, because you are making sacrifices for us by staying in your homes.

We may be apart physically, but we are always together. I really believe in this. These moments are unique – but they can be uniquely special. You cannot be in or around the stadium, or even gather anywhere, today but I can bring you into our dressing-room for a moment, in terms of telling you what we feel as a team.

For us, the importance of what we do and how we do it has never been more critical. For us, it is 'now more than ever'.

Now more than ever, give everything you have. Now more than ever, be brave, but be responsible. Now more than ever, think about how your contribution and effort can help someone other than just yourself. Now more than ever, appreciate the wonderful gift of football and the impact it has. Now more than ever, see the opportunity to create memories and history and embrace it. These games matter now more than ever. And today we have a chance to prove it.

I also think now more than ever we have to embrace the responsibility that those of us blessed to be involved in our sport have, to use this platform of ours for good.

We have seen since our return to playing two important messages on the team shirt and now more than ever these things must be more than just symbols.

For the health workers and all those who serve it, including the care sector, our respect, admiration and appreciation could not be higher. But this must not just be for a short period – it must be constant.

If the applause we gave on those Thursday nights is to mean anything it must be followed up by making sure we never take them for granted again in how they are protected and funded.

For the key workers, the people who kept the shops open and our post delivered and our transport driven and children taught – I could name many more professions who kept working to allow us to shelter – we must value them as much after this as we did during it. It is not allowed to diminish their contribution as 'low-skilled' – they are essential to our society.

And for the Black Lives Matter movement, this must be an opportunity for meaningful change and education, including for people like me, and not just temporary sympathy and outrage.

Now more than ever, we should take forward the causes that really matter to our society and work collectively to improve the world for everyone.

And the final thing to say is specifically for my players, who play at Anfield today for the first time competitively in these new circumstances.

I have never been prouder of them, as professionals and players – but most of all as people. The way they conducted themselves during this defines them more than any performance with a football at their feet.

I appreciate them like crazy all of the time, but after this experience and how they manage it and themselves, it reaches levels I struggle to explain in the English language. Likewise for my incredible staff, but I will speak about them in later columns.

Our players are incredible human beings and I love them from the bottom of my heart. I hope now, more than ever, they get the rewards they deserve on the pitch.

Enjoy the game today and remember: stay safe and support us at home.

Liverpool 4, Crystal Palace 0

Goals: Alexander-Arnold (23), Salah (44), Fabinho (55), Mane (69)

Line-up (4-3-3): Alisson, Alexander-Arnold (Williams 74), Gomez, Van Dijk, Robertson (Elliott 84), Henderson (c) (Oxlade-Chamberlain 64), Fabinho, Wijnaldum, Mane (Keita 84), Firmino (Minamino 74), Salah. Subs not used: Adrian, Lovren, Jones, Origi

Jürgen's post-match reaction: 'We showed a lot, if not everything, that helped us into the position we are in now. What I saw tonight, I wanted to have that before this part of the season and I said to the boys, 'I want to see actually the best behind-closed-doors football ever'. I'm not sure if it was the best football but it was, for sure, the best counter-pressing behind closed doors ever. The attitude we showed tonight, the passion we showed was exceptional and we played some outstanding football. The goals we scored were exceptional. In my job you usually have to calm things down and say, 'No, no that was not that good and we can improve'. And we can improve, I know that, but that's not important tonight. Tonight is only important that we showed our supporters the respect they deserve, that we can play like they are here, even when they are not here. Yes, they can push us to incredible things and without them it's nothing like it is when they are here. And I never missed them more than tonight because imagine this game would have had 55,000 people in the stadium and the emotions which would have then been in the stadium – that would've been incredible. But we cannot have that so it was important that we showed our respect to people and that is what the boys did tonight. I loved it.'

The following night Manchester City lost at Chelsea meaning they could no longer catch the Reds at the top. After a 30-year wait, Liverpool were English champions again. Jürgen gave his reaction:

How does it feel right now?

Good! Pretty good. Honestly, it's still not settled, still not really got it, but it feels brilliant. It was big and it was a wonderful experience. The whole ride is a wonderful experience but especially last night. It was very special. When people spoke about it and thought maybe it's better to win it against City when we play them [next week] on the pitch, but honestly after the 97 points ride last year plus extension with the Champions League, and this season, and all the years before chasing the Champions League spot, I was thinking I want it as early as possible. So, I was completely fine with last night. Honestly, I couldn't feel better. It's just a big relief and it feels like freedom, whatever, I don't know exactly. It's good.

How nice was it that you were all together [watching the Chelsea game on TV]...

So many people would have deserved to be part of this last night. So many more people than there were last night. But we had to make decisions. We all had to make decisions and the decision was everybody who is at Melwood in the moment with us every day and got tested twice can be there, no other people. So we did it without families of course, we did it without the wives as well. It was just the team and the staff around, but that was the minimum that we had to do. You couldn't or I cannot imagine how it would have been had we been all alone at home. Yes, with our families but still kind of alone and not with the players together, how that would have felt. So it was perfect. It was perfectly organised. Nobody had a long time to organise it obviously. We decided to do it after the game against Crystal Palace, we will give it a try. It was big, a big emotional moment. The final whistle was a big moment.

Was it a kind of night when you spoke to the players or did you just want to see them celebrating?

I think it would have been appropriate to speak but I couldn't. I just couldn't. I realised when I started doing the Sky TV interview when the tears came up and then I spoke to Ulla. I had no chance to say a word, I just cried and if I'd have spoken to the players they wouldn't understand me, so it was not the right moment to do that. I have enough opportunities to tell the boys what I think about them and how thankful I am and how much I appreciate the effort they put in, the determination, desire, everything. But they should understand me in that moment and it was not possible last night.

The achievement is just absolutely incredible...
It is and I obviously realised that last night as well. So, 2.30am or around about I was in bed and couldn't sleep. Then everything goes through your mind. Honestly, I know football fans are like this and say now, 'Liverpool is the best team in the world.' I'm not interested in this competition, I'm really not, but I don't think it's possible for any other team in the world to be 20-odd points ahead of Manchester City in a competition like this. Now people say, 'Maybe the league is not that competitive this year.' Well, play it once! Try it. Try and play against Chelsea, play against all the others, play against Leicester City, Burnley, Norwich, Southampton, whatever. Play them and win consistently, that's so incredibly difficult. And the boys, last year 97 points with losing one game to City, then showing up again this year, this consistency is incredible. If I would have an explanation for it, then 100 per cent I should probably write a book about it.

One of your biggest achievements is that the team is the star now, isn't it? It's not about individuals anymore...
It is, but these individuals make a team. It is about individuals and we can't underestimate how influential they all are. But to be really influential you have to realise and to live the team. That means what do you bring in? Last night when we sat together – I think I was

sat together with Trent – if you would give me now a list of five million players, I would love to pick these 25, 30 boys and say I want to do it with them. Because they are so incredibly close, because they understand how important it is to be self-confident on a high, high level but not overly confident that you think you are more important than others. Because without the others, we are nothing – absolutely.

What does the city of Liverpool and its people mean to you?

I said before, this city is obviously music and football. Both things mean emotion. It's just great to do it for these people because you know how much it means to them. Everybody I met now when I came here in the car park, I know what it means to them and I know how hard it is not to celebrate together. These people deserve it so much. I think, how it always is, success in football lifts the mood of the city always and I hope we can use that for the better for all parts which are necessary for this city.

JUL

2020

The Reds had earned seven guards of honour but Klopp was determined that standards wouldn't drop as his relentless squad went in search of records in the final month of the season

2nd: Manchester City (PL) A
5th: Aston Villa (PL) H
8th: Brighton (PL) A
11th: Burnley (PL) H
15th: Arsenal (PL) A
22nd: Chelsea (PL) H
26th: Newcastle (PL) A

Thursday, July 2nd, 8.15pm
Premier League
Manchester City 4, Liverpool 0

Line-up (4-3-3): Alisson, Alexander-Arnold (Williams 76), Gomez (Oxlade-Chamberlain 45), Van Dijk, Robertson, Henderson (c), Fabinho, Wijnaldum (Keita 62), Salah, Firmino (Origi 62), Mane (Minamino 85). Subs not used: Adrian, Milner, Jones, Elliott

Jürgen's post-match reaction: 'It hurts like defeats hurt. What I wanted to see tonight was a team who is ready to fight against Man City, who obviously had, I'm not sure if it's the right saying, a point to prove or whatever. They had easy motivation for Pep, let me say it like this and then the decisive moments, City used and we didn't and that doesn't help. So we had probably more chances than we had in games which we won, but we didn't use them, or none of them, so City were there. Usually we don't give them that many counter-attacks - with two goals they had a throw-in which is a strength of us usually, but tonight it wasn't and that's how it was then and they have this result. Still the surprise is, and it's nice that, in a league where City is playing it's still possible that somebody else can be champion because that's not really likely with the quality they have. We will see how next season [goes], it's a while until then. We still have to play six games until the end of the season. I saw tonight a team which is ready for it, my team, that's absolutely okay.'

v Aston Villa
Sunday, July 5th, 4.30pm

'TITLES DON'T MAKE PLAYERS BETTER. THEIR DAY-TO-DAY WORK DOES THAT'

Premier League

HELLO to you, wherever you are when you read this, ahead of our Premier League fixture against Aston Villa.

Because of the obvious challenges in the region, country and world right now, I am writing this column well before we travel to play Manchester City and therefore cannot reflect upon anything that has happened for us or our opponents since then.

I welcome Dean Smith, the players and officials of Aston Villa to Anfield today. It seems like a lifetime ago that we first met this season, but even given all that time the memories of that unbelievably tough game remain.

Dean has done a fantastic job and his story really is one that makes your heart glow with warmth. He has always been successful whichever club he has managed. And then to have earned the opportunity to lead a club that means so much to him is always good to see.

Their promotion last season was such a big achievement and if I'm being honest the level of performance I see from his side this season says to me they deserve to be in a better position than they find themselves in at the moment.

We know from the game at Villa Park that they can match any side on their day because of their quality and organisation, so we must be ready to work as hard as in any game this season.

Also, my love goes to Dean for the loss he suffered this

season, with his father passing. I was deeply touched by the tribute Aston Villa paid to him and I can only imagine how proud he must have been of his son, achieving something so important and special with the club they both cherish.

Turning back to us, of course this is the first column I have written since we were confirmed champions. I will go into this more ahead of the final home game, because I think it is important to emphasise the need for focus on what we still have ahead of us.

One of our defining features, as a team, has been to embody the spirit of the line in the supporters' song Allez Allez Allez when they declare 'We're never gonna stop'. I love everything about that line.

This team has embraced that mentality. We have achieved much together but we cannot press the pause button for even one moment. It is important to savour and enjoy the special moments. It is not allowed that we don't recognise these shared experiences. But it is possible, if you have the mindset, to do both: enjoy the 'now' but be in a hungry and greedy mood for more in the future.

I keep getting asked about 'dynasty' and 'dominance' and I really don't like it. One headline since we came back wrongly suggested it was our plan to build a dynasty. I never said this and never would.

Let's keep to our values – and that is to be humble.

If we remain humble, as individuals, as a team and as a club, we can achieve so much more together.

And being humble isn't about not celebrating. Trust me, I am a big fan of celebrating like crazy.

Humility is about how you approach your work. For me it's about recognising that I need to improve as a coach and a leader and find ways to be better. For my players it is about being prepared to work even harder than you have before.

Titles don't make players better. Their day-to-day work does that. Their attitude does that, their ability to be humble and accept they are not perfect and can be better. And for our fans it's about recognising that their role will always be critical to everything we do and they need to keep being our energy source.

On that subject, once again our supporters are not able to be at Anfield today but I want to talk about them because not only have they played a vital role in us winning the Premier League, many of them have also responded magnificently to the crisis that the world is in.

Last week I had a Zoom call with some of the Liverpool and Everton fans who worked together to produce personal protective equipment when there was a national shortage.

What they have done is unbelievable. To want to respond in that way is more than good enough in itself, but to have the ingenuity, determination and leadership to make it happen on a mass scale is so incredible that I could not possibly find the words to do it justice.

I felt privileged to speak to them. They are heroes. By finding ingenious ways to support our community locally they have undoubtedly helped save lives and keep people safe. This, to me, is the spirit of Liverpool. It is why I have come to love the city and its people.

I also want to pay tribute to the supporters who volunteered to deliver food to some of the most vulnerable members of our community. I am told that this was organised by the Spirit Of Shankly and there is no doubt that by acting in this way they lived up to the spirit of one of the greatest men of all.

But it is knowing that so many of you have done so much at a time of great suffering that made last Friday's events at the Pier Head so disappointing. I am a football manager, not a judge, and I have the same ability to make the mistakes of a human being as everyone else, so what I am saying should be taken in this spirit. But I also have to be clear: what we saw was not good for Liverpool the city or Liverpool the club.

The same people who were vulnerable when supporters were manufacturing PPE and delivering food are still vulnerable now. We cannot allow all of this brilliant work to go to waste because some have decided that they either cannot wait for a celebration or that

COVID-19 is no longer a threat. If we do this, people – our people – will be put at risk.

We need you to stay at home as much as possible, not because we want to stop your enjoyment, but because we care for everyone who lives in this city and other places beyond.

It is a strange thing for me to say because it goes against everything that I usually would say, but right now we do not want to see you at stadiums and we don't want to see you gathering to celebrate. I say this out of a sense of care and for no other reason.

When the time comes you will be back at Anfield and we will also be able to celebrate together. I cannot wait for these moments, but the time is not now. We must respect the virus like we would respect any opponent. Anything else puts all of us at risk.

If we can all follow the example of our supporters who have put others first, we will not go wrong and we owe it to ourselves to do that.

Liverpool 2, Aston Villa 0

Goals: Mane (71), Jones (89)

Line-up (4-3-3): Alisson, Alexander-Arnold, Gomez, Van Dijk (c), Robertson (Williams 90+4), Oxlade-Chamberlain (Wijnaldum 61), Fabinho (Henderson 61), Keita (Jones 85), Salah, Origi (Firmino 61), Mane. Subs not used: Adrian, Minamino, Shaqiri, Elliott

Jürgen's post-match reaction: 'It's easy, if we want to have a record points tally we pretty much have to win all the football games so it's not that complicated - I don't have to mention it, the boys know that. But it's not necessary for this group, we played for everything each three days, for the three points, because you don't get any more how ever good you play. You get three points if you win and that's enough and I saw that again today. These boys are really fighting for these three points in a very difficult game. I think we should have had, in the first half, a shot on target because it should have been a penalty on Mo Salah, to be honest. But it was a difficult game, Aston Villa did really well and now everybody will be really happy that I mentioned it but the wind was again really tricky. I see a few of you sitting in the stands with winter coats and on the pitch the wind in the far right corner was incredible. I'm not sure who from Aston Villa tried to shoot the ball as far as he can and it came pretty much straight back. One reason, the wind [itself] and another reason, it dries the pitch like crazy and it means the pitch was really difficult. If you have the ball and you want to play then it's difficult, if you cannot play on the ground but want to go with long balls [then] the wind doesn't help with that. So it's better that you are the not-dominant team in these situations and we had a few problems, but I liked how we stayed in the game, how we tried to find solutions. We tried really to adapt and I saw the improvement on the pitch, and then of course when the fresh players came on it was easier for them with fresh legs against a team that was already really busy. It's just an intense period - we will go through that but we need to make smart decisions.'

Wednesday, July 8th, 8.15pm
Premier League
Brighton 1, Liverpool 3

Goals: Salah (6, 76), Henderson (8)

Line-up (4-3-3): Alisson, Alexander-Arnold, Gomez, Van Dijk, Williams (Robertson 45), Keita (Fabinho 61), Henderson (c) (Milner 80), Wijnaldum, Oxlade-Chamberlain (Mane 61), Firmino (Minamino 87), Salah. Subs not used: Adrian, Origi, Jones, Elliott

Jürgen's post-match reaction: 'It was a difficult game against a good opponent, a deserved win. Job done, job well done in big parts of the game but not in all. That's how it is. I think we started really, really well, we finished really, really well, but in between we left the door a bit too wide open for Brighton. But only because Brighton was really good; they played really good football, took some risks in the formation. Some of them were really threatening counter-attacks so we had to block twice in the box. The goals we scored tonight, they were really good. We had a lot to move to score the goals, so that's nice. We could have scored more, that's true, but that's pretty much all. Two-hundred-and-fifty goals [between Salah, Firmino and Mane] is really exceptional – imagine where I would be if these boys did not play for me! Wow! The situation minus 250 goals… great!'

Post-match notes

Neco Williams made his first Premier League start, while this was the Reds' 13th away league win of the season – the joint most the club has ever achieved.

v Burnley
Saturday, July 11th, 3pm

'MONEY DOES NOT HEAL A SERIOUS INJURY AND THE GAME WITHOUT PLAYERS IS NOTHING'

HELLO to you, wherever you are when you read this, ahead of our Premier League fixture against Burnley.

I welcome Sean Dyche, his players, staff and officials of our visitors to Anfield for the match today.

What an incredible job Sean has done again this season. My respect and admiration could not be higher. I know from my own experiences that operating in the top-flight of a hugely competitive league, with limited budget and resources, is a massive challenge and tests all your skills as a coach and leader.

Each season I am here in England, Burnley progresses and probably now some people don't give this the credit it deserves. I look at the league table and where they are and I think 'another miracle performed'. Sean and Burnley are a real success story in the Premier League.

I think I have said before, as opponents, as managers, we don't really 'know' each other. We meet a couple of times a season when we play against each other and occasionally at league [managers] meetings.

On the touchline you would probably think we do not like each other, but that is the heat of battle. Away from there – wow – what I think about him is highest level.

During the pandemic we had a number of Zoom meetings as managers and I really love Sean's personality and humour. You can see why his players give their all for him.

For me Burnley are one of the teams of this season

and I hope they get the recognition they deserve, because inside the game, among managers and coaches and players, the respect could not be greater for them as a team.

Turning back to today's match, we are currently in the midst of a really intensive schedule matches-wise and this does pose challenges. To be clear, this is not an excuse even for one second. The same applies to our opponent today, so it's not about the game. It is about player welfare and player safety.

Again, to be clear, I am not silly and I know we are in extraordinary times and that we all have to make sacrifices to complete our season. I also get that when compared to the challenges the rest of society faces, our problems are luxury problems. So I do not speak about this for sympathy and I do not look to offer an excuse for any result or performance.

I also appreciate the great efforts that so many in football have gone to in order to make competitive games possible.

However, I also have a responsibility to my players to look after their health and wellbeing and sometimes that means speaking out, even if I personally attract criticism from those who choose to misrepresent my position.

The issue isn't playing one game in quick succession after another. This is our life and we are used to it. If you have to play Wednesday and Saturday during a season, we can all deal with this.

But when it comes after a period where you have been asked to do this constantly it adds up and it has an impact. Impact on muscles and bones and energy – and concentration. Players at this level are privileged, yes, in terms of the rewards given. But the human body isn't insulated from injury by wages. It's about load and this schedule increases the risk of injury.

I am not saying anything in this column that I haven't said directly to the person at the Premier League responsible for the schedule. I know that they do the best they can in unbelievably difficult circumstances, now more than ever.

I know to a certain extent it is an impossible job. But I hope that – as an industry – we look at how it impacts on the players' health.

The end of this season is what it is and we all have to do what we can to make the best of it. Again, it's not just a Liverpool problem, it's a problem for all teams and all players.

Going forward, if the next season is also to be impacted because of the disruption caused by this virus, we must all come together to find a better solution and a fair solution.

I personally don't think it is right to play Thursday-Sunday-Wednesday-Saturday as we have been asked, particularly when the third game in that sequence is the latest kick-off in a part of the country as far away from our home as possible. Again, not an excuse and it is not about results, but it is an issue to address for the sake of the players' health.

Once again, I do not think one person or one organisation is responsible for a solution – we all are.

The clubs and their owners, the league, the other federations, and – yes, not a popular thing to say with the media – but the TV companies also.

I believe there is an English phrase about 'biting the hand that feeds you' and having worked for broadcasters earlier in my career in Germany I appreciate as much as anyone the positive impact they have on our industry and how they fund it. But, again, money does not heal a serious injury and the game without players is nothing.

So, with the schedule likely to be a challenge for next season and beyond, I hope we can all maybe put aside some self-interest and ask what can we do to allow our players to be able to perform without placing undue risk on their safety?

There are enough intelligent, thoughtful people in the process to find a solution that works, so let's do it together.

In an attempt to avoid any risk of my words being misinterpreted I will say that again: let's do it together.

It isn't about one league, one club, one group or one

individual. It is about all of us working together for the good of football and footballers. I am sure that we can all agree that this would be in the best interests of us all.

Finishing with a message directly to our supporters, I would like to thank them for the incredible responsibility they showed for our last home game.

I did not like having to refer to incidents I saw and was disappointed in. I think LFC fans know the regard I hold them in.

But what is great, is that having had the messages from people far smarter than me – such as Matthew Ashton who is in charge of public health in Liverpool – they listened and they acted.

Mr Ashton joined our press conference before we played Villa and I thanked him and his staff during that for all they do, and all the health workers and those in the care section in our society.

But we can show our thanks best through our actions. Let's keep listening to the real experts – people like Matthew Ashton – and let's keep our city and region as safe as possible during this difficult time.

Liverpool 1, Burnley 1

Goal: Robertson (34)

Line-up (4-3-3): Alisson, Williams (Alexander-Arnold 69), Gomez, Van Dijk (c), Robertson, Wijnaldum (Oxlade-Chamberlain 81), Fabinho, Jones (Keita 69), Mane, Firmino, Salah. Subs not used: Adrian, Lovren, Minamino, Shaqiri, Origi, Elliott.

Jürgen's post-match reaction: 'It was a good performance in most parts of the game. There were moments when it was like Liverpool against Nick Pope. I think it's the biggest challenge in football to play against a team which is that well organised and create against a team that is that well organised and has such an outstanding attitude like Burnley has. But we created super chances but there was one guy who wanted to deny us and that was Nick Pope. That was then the problem pretty much of the game because for different reasons this result left the door open for Burnley. It was always clear they had corners where Ali was really under pressure from three or four players around. Then free-kicks on top of that, not too much but some. It was clear they want to have these situations. When they had them it was always a threat. Apart from that, how I said, we really did well, we should have scored more but we didn't do that. I'm fine with the performance for 80 minutes, I would say. More than fine because it was probably one of the best games we played against Burnley but we didn't score and that's why we only got a point.'

Post-match notes

This draw halted a run of 24 Premier League wins at Anfield in a row but the Reds had now gone 58 consecutive matches without defeat in the league at home.

Wednesday, July 15th, 8.15pm
Premier League
Arsenal 2, Liverpool 1

Goal: Mane (20)

Line-up (4-3-3): Alisson, Alexander-Arnold, Gomez, Van Dijk (c), Robertson, Wijnaldum (Shaqiri 83), Fabinho, Oxlade-Chamberlain (Keita 61), Firmino (Minamino 61), Salah (Origi 83), Mane. Subs not used: Adrian, Lovren, Williams, Jones, Elliott

Jürgen's post-match reaction: 'We were very dominant, a lot of good football. In the end, why are we in the situation we are? Because we are a very good football team and we usually work on a concentration level that is nearly unhuman. Today we made some human errors, which is not so nice but not completely surprising that it can happen. Tonight it happened. Usually we learn from situations like this, we will do that now again. The boys don't want to hide or say, 'It's not my fault' or whatever, that's all clear on the table. But around that, I don't think I ever played a game with 24 to three shots against Arsenal. There are a lot of goals usually when we play against each other, but not that many tonight – at least on our side. But that dominance we never had before. So I'm happy about that. We will carry on and then the concentration level, we expect that we are always there. In two situations we were obviously not there but we have to take that now and when we learn from it we will be fine.'

v Chelsea
Wednesday, July 22nd, 8.15pm

'THIS IS OUR MOMENT. WE HAVE ALL EARNED IT. SO EMBRACE IT AND CHERISH IT'

Premier League

HELLO to you wherever you are when you read this, ahead of our final Premier League fixture at Anfield this season against Chelsea.

I welcome Frank Lampard, his players, staff and officials of the visitors to our home.

What a job Frank has done this season. We have played them three times already this campaign, in three different competitions and each time the games have been so close and so tight. They are already starting to reflect their manager's personality in how they approach the game and it's very easy to see they are heading in the right direction.

Wonderful players, some really smart and ambitious recruitments made, superb leadership in the manager's office. Chelsea have been a real challenge this season and will be even stronger next.

Moving to ourselves, as much as the 90 minutes is the main focus, I cannot ignore the hugely significant night we are about to experience as a team and as a club.

Yes, as always the game comes first and all our attention and energies will be on that. We have a responsibility to the competition, of course, but also ourselves. We have enjoyed a wonderful season and it is important we finish it in a manner fitting the level of achievement. This is something within our control. As we have all season, we set our own standards and try to exceed them.

I know I won't need to remind the players of this,

because they are smart and hungry and they know the job to do.

When the game is done, we will be recognised as Champions of England. The first time since 1990 for this incredible football club.

I know we live in a world where 'what's next' often. means the 'here and now' isn't savoured as much as it should be. No sooner had we been confirmed Champions – on the night when tonight's opponents had beaten Manchester City – and the questions were coming about 'legacy' and 'winning more'.

It is so important to enjoy the wonderful moments when they come. And this is one of those. I don't normally like referencing the length of time Liverpool has endured before claiming this title, because so often when working to clinch it my message was to ignore the weight of that gap. Last season, when we came so close, I said to the players afterwards that this was not the 29th attempt for them – for us, it was our first proper one. I also told them I loved them, appreciated them and was so proud to be able to call myself their manager.

Everything I said in the dressing-room after Wolves at home last season when we came so close but ultimately could only achieve runners up, applies now but even more so.

I could not love this group of players more. I could not appreciate them more. I could not be more proud of them. This achievement is their achievement. Their focus. Their dedication. Their talent. Their hunger. That's what has delivered this title. They sacrificed, individually and collectively, and they have their rewards.

This group of players are giants for what they achieved. They have earned every bit of praise and adulation that has come their way.

Tonight is their moment as a team and even though it is happening in unique circumstances, the magnitude of what they have delivered stands alongside some of the greatest sides ever to grace our home.

Typically I have used a lot of words there to express a sentiment I could have summed up in just two: 'thank you'. Thank you to the most incredible football team any manager could be privileged to lead. The same applies to two other special groups, my remarkable staff and the Liverpool supporters.

This is a moment in the column where I have to show discipline, because if I start naming too many of the 'team behind the team' I risk leaving people out who deserve recognition – and to name everyone who deserves it would take up most of the programme.

Needless to say, without this extraordinary group I would be nothing. They support me, they educate me, they inspire me and they give me energy and drive. It isn't just the coaching staff either. Of course these are the guys I spend the most time with and have the biggest influence on team matters.

But it's so much wider.

Every person who walks through the gates of Melwood makes our environment the place it is. They all contribute.

And not 'big or small' – only big, only important, only critical. They do the hard lifting in the shadows and allow the team and people like myself to enjoy the sunshine when times are good. But we know their value and they are as worthy of the title 'Champions' as anyone I can think of.

I did say it isn't right or possible to list names but there are two I simply must: Pepijn Lijnders and Peter Krawietz.

Both are world-class coaches and leaders in their own right. They have driven this team forward with their brains, knowledge and imagination. I could not be more appreciative of their contribution. I will forever be grateful.

Our supporters too, although absent since the season re-started, remain the wind in our sails. It is impossible to sum up their impact or their importance. They are the reason that representing this club brings the greatest possible emotional attachment and therefore emotional reward. What we do here we do together. At times that has meant suffering together. But right now – and in the last 14 months – it has meant celebrating together. I love this.

It would not mean as much were it not for our supporters. They might not be in Anfield tonight in person but their spirit can be felt and we lift this trophy for them.

It has been their wait, their anguish, their dreams. I hope wherever in our city, region, the country or the world they watch from, they realise it is they that make LFC the club with the biggest heart and the most joyful soul in world sport.

Before moving to something more personal I must acknowledge our brilliant owners and football operations team. For FSG, unable to be here tonight because of the current global crisis, this title should act as vindication for smart and brave decisions made over the course of a decade.

Mike Gordon specifically. He is my friend as well as my 'boss'. He is the embodiment of the word 'supportive' - such a special guy – and he made this happen. He and John, Tom and FSG should be very proud tonight. And to Michael Edwards and his team likewise – incredibly smart people who have made nothing but outstanding decisions. This is fulfilment of a vision.

And finally, for this season, this very special campaign, I must say the words 'thank you' to the people who bring me the most joy of all. My family.

My wife Ulla who is my best friend on this planet. I love you so much. My two sons, Marc and Dennis, you have only ever brought me joy and a feeling of pride. What incredible men you have become. To see you grow as people beats any other achievement in life.

Doing this crazy job is fun because of these three people – my wife and my boys. The bad times are softened and the good times sweetened because we live through them together, as our own 'team'. They are my everything and my heart is constantly filled with love and happiness because of them. I feel so blessed to have a situation where I am surrounded by people, personally and professionally, who make me realise what a wonderful gift life is.

The times we live in in this moment test us all. For some, the test is unfair and too much to bear. I know we are living through a period where for many joy must feel like a horizon you cannot reach or see. But I hope for the Liverpool family, what we have collectively experienced this season brings some warmth and comfort.

Tonight, when we end a 30-year wait, know that in that moment we will all experience something special and we will experience it together. If nothing else, this is the true beauty of our game and of this club.

This is our moment. We have all earned it. So embrace it and cherish it.

Thank you.

Liverpool 5, Chelsea 3

Goals: Keita (23), Alexander-Arnold (38), Wijnaldum (43), Firmino (54), Oxlade-Chamberlain (84)

Line-up (4-3-3): Alisson, Alexander-Arnold, Gomez, Van Dijk (c), Robertson, Keita (Jones 66), Fabinho, Wijnaldum (Milner 66), Salah (Oxlade-Chamberlain 79), Firmino (Minamino 87), Mane (Origi 87). Subs not used: Adrian, Lovren, Lallana, Shaqiri

Jürgen's post-match reaction: 'The boys gave us the opportunity to have a really special night. A lot of people before the game thought one team is fighting for the Champions League while the other is maybe on the beach but these boys are so special. I couldn't be more proud. It was an open game but there were nice goals with super footballing moments. I loved the game, so we could enjoy the rest of the night. It's a great moment. It's all about consistency. We had to earn that, it's all about staying greedy. I can say in a pre-match meeting whatever I want - 'you want to win you have to work hard, Chelsea are too good'. I'm surprised myself, how can you put in a shift like that when you're thinking 'I want to be fine afterwards'. I was angry during the game and it was my plan not to be angry! Tonight it was very difficult because Chelsea was so good but the boys did it anyway.'

Post-match notes

This win moved Liverpool on to 96 points, a poignant number as Sir Kenny Dalglish took part in the trophy presentation ceremony on the Kop.

Sunday, July 26th, 4pm
Premier League
Newcastle United 1, Liverpool 3

Goals: Van Dijk (38), Origi (59), Mane (89)

Line-up (4-3-3): Alisson, Williams (Alexander-Arnold 85), Gomez, Van Dijk, Robertson, Keita (Jones 85), Milner (c), Wijnaldum, Oxlade-Chamberlain (Firmino 64), Origi (Salah 64), Minamino (Mane 64). Subs not used: Adrian, Fabinho, Shaqiri, Elliott

Jürgen's post-match reaction: 'It was the target for the day, to finish it on a high and we did it. We got a little wake-up call and from that moment on the boys worked really hard to play against this defensive wall of Newcastle. We made five changes and brought on fresh legs again and that helped, obviously. Then we controlled the game completely and I liked it a lot. It was not perfect, but like our season, the boys don't only win games on the perfect days, they are ready to really dig deep on the not-so-perfect days and that's what I really like. Sixty minutes' rest helped [the regular front three], obviously, but it was exactly right and the other boys did the hard work before. A victory of the whole squad, how the whole season [was]'

Post-match notes

Liverpool finished on 99 points, the highest total in the club's history.

NOW YOU'RE GONNA BELIEVE US...

Relief and ecstasy were the overriding emotions as, many months after an extraordinary journey began, we got to see Liverpool lift the Premier League trophy. It was a time for joy and reflection for the boss

Klopp on the trophy presentation...

It was absolutely great, absolutely great. It made it even more special that the families could be in the stadium. They were not allowed for the game, but for the trophy lift it was allowed. We knew they were in the stadium, but because of the lights we didn't see them, but I knew my family – which I didn't see for a pretty long time – was here tonight, which made it even more special because you want to share these moments with loved ones. All my loved ones were around me with the players, the staff and the people I work with. My family means a lot to me, so it was really, really special in that moment. I loved the moment – and the boys did. It's strange, you stand on a stage and there is nobody – not nobody, but not as many as you would imagine in a situation like that – but I have to say, the people who organised it made the best of it. If it would have been the last game – win today and we are champions – then we wouldn't have had the opportunity to go on the Kop. I was never on the Kop before, it was pretty special and I think it makes sense in the moment when the people are not in that we use the Kop to celebrate it with them together in our hearts. It was really good.

Klopp on his team's consistency...

It's all about consistency. When we started we had these great games of football and then the next game it was different. We had to work on that. It's about having a high level in training. Everyone deserves a medal. We play like we play because we train like we train.

Klopp on the drive for more success...

We are champions of England, Europe and the world. It is unbelievable but it's true. I couldn't be more proud. We need the pictures (of all the trophies) for while it lasts. Because it doesn't happen too often. But we will not stop. We have internal challenges. We can improve each player. Naby (Keita) played only the last part of the season. We have a chance to make another step. The others will not sleep. Chelsea are such a talented team. There are all the others, Manchester United and Man City.

Klopp on his players' desire...

Winning trophies doesn't make it easier to win more but at least it gives you the proof that it's possible. If you open Pandora's Box that helps massively. I could see that when we won the Champions League last year that made all the other things happen. Ninety seven points and winning the Champions League is really a special year. Some people told me the reaction of the boys was really special but I think the reaction was like it should be. If you are that close you just have to invest more and you can get over the line, and that is exactly what happened. We will stay greedy, we have to. If that then leads automatically to more trophies, I don't know because other teams have other reasons to make the next step. We will not change our attitude. We will try to improve everything. The boys have written a really nice story over the last few years but it's not over yet. We will decide when it's finished. I just want to see us fighting for the next trophy, enjoying the hard work. As long as we do that, we have a good chance. We have to be a team nobody wants to play against. We are a little bit like this but we can be even more uncomfortable to play and that is what we have to try.

Klopp's message to the fans...

What can I say? Five years ago I asked you to change from doubters to believers and you did it. You made it happen. Savour it and drink what you want. But you have to prepare for a party. When? I don't know. When this virus is gone then we will have it.

Klopp summing up the season...

The football part of the year was exceptional, absolutely exceptional, 99 points. After having 97 last year, this is absolutely exceptional. The boys showed a consistency that is really second to none and that's what we had to do, we knew that. It was clear that if you want to win against them [Manchester City] and be ahead of them, you need to be nearly perfect. The boys were nearly perfect and that's why we have 99 points. It will have a special place in my own memories, for sure.

SEASON STATISTICS

The numbers that helped Jürgen Klopp's men set such a staggering pace in a unique season

Appearances (all competitions)

Name	*PL*	*FA*	*LC*	*Europe*	*Other*	*Total*
Roberto Firmino	*38*	*2*	*0*	*9*	*3*	*52*
Virgil Van Dijk	*38*	*1*	*0*	*9*	*2*	*50*
Trent Alexander-Arnold	*38*	*0*	*0*	*8*	*3*	*49*
Andy Robertson	*36*	*1*	*0*	*9*	*3*	*49*
Mohamed Salah	*34*	*2*	*0*	*9*	*3*	*48*
Sadio Mané	*35*	*1*	*0*	*9*	*2*	*47*
Georginio Wijnaldum	*37*	*0*	*0*	*9*	*1*	*47*
Alex Oxlade-Chamberlain	*30*	*2*	*2*	*6*	*3*	*43*
Joe Gomez	*28*	*2*	*2*	*8*	*3*	*43*
Divock Origi	*28*	*3*	*1*	*7*	*3*	*42*
Jordan Henderson	*30*	*0*	*0*	*7*	*3*	*40*
Fabinho Tavarez	*28*	*2*	*0*	*8*	*1*	*39*
Alisson Becker	*29*	*0*	*0*	*5*	*3*	*37*
James Milner	*22*	*2*	*2*	*9*	*2*	*37*
Naby Keita	*18*	*0*	*2*	*4*	*3*	*27*
Adam Lallana	*15*	*2*	*2*	*0*	*3*	*22*
Adrián San Miguel	*11*	*3*	*0*	*4*	*0*	*18*
Dejan Lovren	*10*	*1*	*1*	*3*	*0*	*15*
Takumi Minamino	*10*	*3*	*0*	*1*	*0*	*14*
Joël Matip	*9*	*1*	*0*	*2*	*1*	*13*
Curtis Jones	*6*	*4*	*2*	*0*	*0*	*12*
Xherdan Shaqiri	*7*	*0*	*0*	*1*	*3*	*11*
Neco Williams	*6*	*4*	*1*	*0*	*0*	*11*
Harvey Elliott	*2*	*3*	*3*	*0*	*0*	*8*
Pedro Chirivella	*0*	*3*	*3*	*0*	*0*	*6*
Caoimhin Kelleher	*0*	*1*	*3*	*0*	*0*	*4*
Sepp van den Berg	*0*	*1*	*3*	*0*	*0*	*4*
Ki-Jana Hoever	*0*	*1*	*2*	*0*	*0*	*3*
Rhian Brewster	*0*	*1*	*2*	*0*	*0*	*3*
Herbie Kane	*0*	*0*	*2*	*0*	*0*	*2*

Yasser Larouci	*0*	*2*	*0*	*0*	*0*	*2*
Leighton Clarkson	*0*	*1*	*1*	*0*	*0*	*2*
Morgan Boyes	*0*	*1*	*1*	*0*	*0*	*2*
Tony Gallacher	*0*	*0*	*1*	*0*	*0*	*1*
Elijah Dixon-Bonner	*0*	*1*	*0*	*0*	*0*	*1*
Jack Bearne	*0*	*0*	*1*	*0*	*0*	*1*
James Norris	*0*	*0*	*1*	*0*	*0*	*1*
Thomas Hill	*0*	*0*	*1*	*0*	*0*	*1*
Nathaniel Phillips	*0*	*1*	*0*	*0*	*0*	*1*
Liam Millar	*0*	*1*	*0*	*0*	*0*	*1*
Joe Hardy	*0*	*1*	*0*	*0*	*0*	*1*
Jake Cain	*0*	*1*	*0*	*0*	*0*	*1*
Adam Lewis	*0*	*1*	*0*	*0*	*0*	*1*
Luis Longstaff	*0*	*0*	*1*	*0*	*0*	*1*
Isaac Christie-Davies	*0*	*0*	*1*	*0*	*0*	*1*

Selection of milestones from the 2019-20 season:

– Best ever start to a season by any team in Europe's top five leagues (61 points from 21 games)

– Most successive Premier League home wins (24, continuing from 2018-19 season)

– Every league opponent beaten in the same season

– Fastest to 30 wins in a single season (34 matches)

– Most points accumulated over 38 matches (110, after the 3-2 win against West Ham, continuing from 2018-19 season)

– Premier League won in fewest games (31)

– Biggest ever lead in England's top division (25 points)

Goals (all competitions)

Name	*PL*	*FA*	*LC*	*Europe*	*Other*	*Total*
Mohamed Salah	*19*	*0*	*0*	*4*	*0*	*23*
Sadio Mané	*18*	*0*	*0*	*4*	*0*	*22*
Roberto Firmino	*9*	*0*	*0*	*1*	*2*	*12*
Alex Oxlade-Chamberlain	*4*	*0*	*1*	*3*	*0*	*8*
Divock Origi	*4*	*0*	*2*	*0*	*0*	*6*
Georginio Wijnaldum	*4*	*0*	*0*	*2*	*0*	*6*
Own goals	*2*	*2*	*1*	*0*	*0*	*5*
Virgil Van Dijk	*5*	*0*	*0*	*0*	*0*	*5*
Trent Alexander-Arnold	*4*	*0*	*0*	*0*	*0*	*4*
Naby Keita	*2*	*0*	*0*	*1*	*1*	*4*
Jordan Henderson	*4*	*0*	*0*	*0*	*0*	*4*
James Milner	*2*	*0*	*2*	*0*	*0*	*4*
Andy Robertson	*2*	*0*	*0*	*1*	*0*	*3*
Curtis Jones	*1*	*2*	*0*	*0*	*0*	*3*
Joël Matip	*1*	*0*	*0*	*0*	*1*	*2*
Fabinho Tavarez	*2*	*0*	*0*	*0*	*0*	*2*
Dejan Lovren	*0*	*0*	*0*	*1*	*0*	*1*
Ki-Jana Hoever	*0*	*0*	*1*	*0*	*0*	*1*
Adam Lallana	*1*	*0*	*0*	*0*	*0*	*1*
Xherdan Shaqiri	*1*	*0*	*0*	*0*	*0*	*1*

Players transferred in for/during 2019-20 season

Sepp van den Berg	*PEC Zwolle*	*June 2019*
Harvey Elliott	*Fulham*	*July 2019*
Adrian San Miguel	*Free*	*August 2019*
Andy Lonergan	*Free*	*August 2019*
Takumi Minamino	*Red Bull Salzburg*	*January 2020*

Trophies

Premier League
UEFA European Super Cup
FIFA Club World Cup

Premier League Manager of the Month awards

Jürgen Klopp	*August*
	September
	November
	December
	January

Premier League Player of the Month awards

November	*Sadio Mane*
December	*Trent Alexander-Arnold*

Selection of milestones from the 2019-20 season:

– Liverpool finish on 99 points, the highest total in the club's history

– 14 away league wins is the most the club have ever achieved in one season

– For the first time, the Reds remained unbeaten in the league at Anfield for a third consecutive season

– The Reds earned 13 league doubles in a season for the first time

Liverpool FC Premier League 2019-20 statistics

Most passes

Virgil 3,259
Robbo 2,492
Trent 2,440
Joe 1,988
Hendo 1,856

Most assists

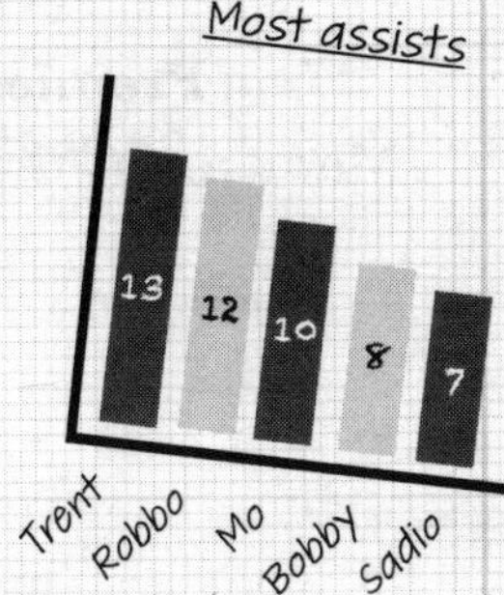

Most tackles

Hendo 63
Fabinho 62
Trent 55
Robbo 54
Sadio 44

Minutes played

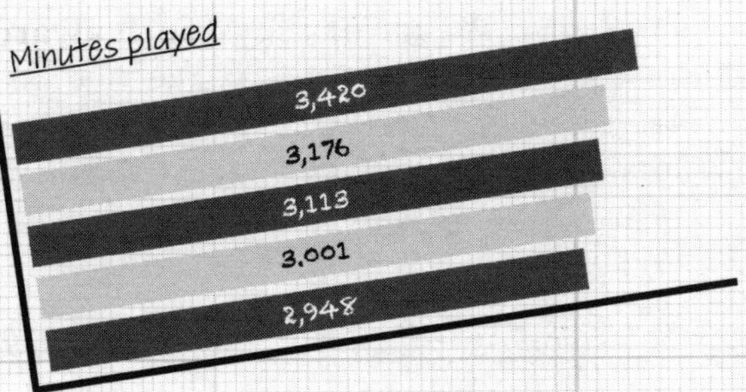

Appearances

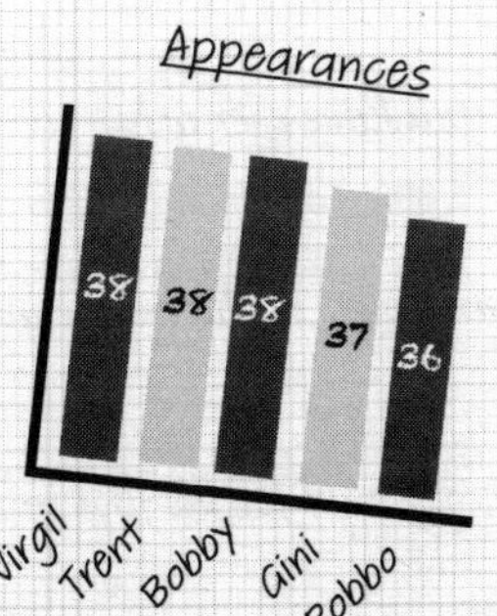

Goalscorers

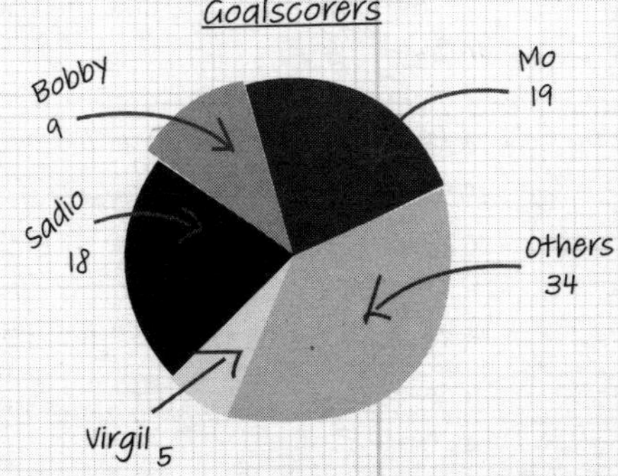

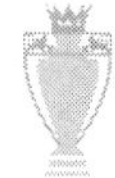

Final Premier League table 2019-20 season

	P	W	D	L	F	A	GD	Pts
1 Liverpool	**38**	**32**	**3**	**3**	**85**	**33**	**52**	**99**
2 Manchester City	38	26	3	9	102	35	67	81
3 Manchester United	38	18	12	8	66	36	30	66
4 Chelsea	38	20	6	12	69	54	15	66
5 Leicester City	38	18	8	12	67	41	26	62
6 Tottenham	38	16	11	11	61	47	14	59
7 Wolverhampton W	38	15	14	9	51	40	11	59
8 Arsenal	38	14	14	10	56	48	8	56
9 Sheffield United	38	14	12	12	39	39	0	54
10 Burnley	38	15	9	14	43	50	-7	54
11 Southampton	38	15	7	16	51	60	-9	52
12 Everton	38	13	10	15	44	56	-12	49
13 Newcastle United	38	11	11	16	38	58	-20	44
14 Crystal Palace	38	11	10	17	31	50	-19	43
15 Brighton	38	9	14	15	39	54	-15	41
16 West Ham	38	10	9	19	49	62	-13	39
17 Aston Villa	38	9	8	21	41	67	-26	35
18 AFC Bournemouth	38	9	7	22	40	65	-25	34
19 Watford	38	8	10	20	36	64	-28	34
20 Norwich	38	5	6	27	26	75	-49	21